Favorite Recipes

from Famous Restaurants

In the United States and Canada

Volume 6

Recipes compiled and tested by

Nancy Kennedy

Women's Editor, Ford Times

Ford Motor Company          Dearborn, Michigan

# FOREWORD

It's always nice to be associated with a winner. And, quite obviously, we have one in our "Favorite Recipes from Famous Restaurants" feature that appears in *Ford Times* each month.

*Ford Times* readers like it. Many have written or called to tell us so. What's more, they have been just as favorable in their comments to representatives of the independent research firms that periodically make reader surveys for us. Finally, the feature that has distinguished the pages of *Ford Times* for the last 30 years has been paid the ultimate publishing compliment: It has been copied by other publications.

The coverage has proved equally popular when compiled into book form. Over the years, we have published five cookbooks totaling nearly one million copies. All five volumes have been sellouts and are now out of print.

We are pleased to bring you this sixth *Ford Times* cookbook to add to your dining pleasure at home and on the road. You'll note that we have not tampered with the tried-and-true format. This book is larger and the cover more colorful, but otherwise you'll find few changes from our earlier books.

Included are the most prized recipes from more than 200 popular restaurants in the United States and Canada—restaurants that have not been in any of our earlier volumes. Each restaurant is illustrated by a painting, photo or line drawing, assuring that this book—like the first five—will be used by art classes as well as family chefs and chauffeurs.

We trust you will find this volume worthy of placing beside the other *Ford Times* cookbooks, whether in your kitchen or car.

*The Editors*

**ABOUT THE COVER**

One of the pleasantest aspects of travel in the United States is the tremendous variety and excellence of the foods that can be enjoyed along the way. A seascape by Alphonse Shelton provides the background for this still life of American delicacies.

Book design by Jerry L. Anderson
Photographic art direction by Leonard P. Johnson
Editorial assistance by Mary Zimmer
Photography by Don Rockhey

# Contents

# Northeast

This is a region with an exciting array of foods, from the sophisticated menus of its metropolitan restaurants to the simpler, but satisfying, dishes of rustic resorts deep in the New England woods. A seascape by Gilbert Di Cicco is the background for some of the seafoods, fruits, vegetables and wine that sustain a Yankee tradition of plain foods made memorable by deft cooking.

9

# The Weather Vane

"Cooking is an art," says Clelia De Maio who has operated this restaurant for 38 years. All of the baking is done in the kitchen; vegetables are cooked in small quantities and the food is served with great style. Open for lunch and dinner every day except Monday at 4137 Whitney Avenue, Hamden, Connecticut (9 miles north of New Haven).

## CINNAMON ROLLS OR BREAD

Scald 1½ cups of milk. Add 2 tbsp. sugar, 1 tsp. salt and ⅓ cup melted butter. Cool to lukewarm. Soften 3 yeast cakes (or 3 envelopes of dry yeast) according to package directions. Stir well and add to milk. Add 1 well-beaten egg. Mix in about 5 cups of all-purpose flour to make dough that is easy to handle but not too stiff. Brush dough with melted butter and put in a warm place until it rises to twice its bulk.

Roll out dough to ¼-inch thickness. Brush with melted butter. Sprinkle with 1 cup of brown sugar and ¼ cup cinnamon. Roll up like a jelly roll and cut into 36 slices.

For bread, divide roll into 3 parts. Place on greased baking tin. Let rise again to twice its bulk. Bake rolls in 375° to 400° oven for 10 minutes. Bake loaves at same temperature, but for 30 to 35 minutes. Brush them with butter as they come from oven.

# The Yankee Silversmith

This charming country inn was established in 1953 on the site of the Yale and Hough homesteads in the heart of America's silverware country. Innkeeper Robert Meyer can now be host to 600 diners at one time in the dining rooms which are open every day for lunch and dinner. Closed December 24, 25 and 26. On U.S. 5, in Wallingford, Connecticut, the inn may be reached by taking Exit 66 from the Wilbur Cross-Merritt Parkway, or Exit 15 from I-91. Reservations suggested.

## CASSEROLES OF BAKED LOBSTER FOR TWO

Into each of 2 individual ramekins put 1/16 tsp. of crushed garlic and 1 tbsp. butter. Then top each with 6 oz. boiled lobster meat in chunks. Cover with Cheddar Stuffing (above).

*Cheddar Stuffing:* Combine 1½ cups fresh bread crumbs; 2 oz. grated Cheddar cheese; ⅛ tsp. paprika and 4 oz. melted butter. Pour over lobster meat and place in 375° oven for 20 minutes until brown. Put under broiler to finish browning the top of the stuffing. Just before serving sprinkle 1 oz. dry sherry over the tops. Serves 2.

# The Mayflower Inn

Nestled in the Berkshire foothills, just 90 miles from New York and 125 miles from Boston, this old-fashioned country inn re-creates the mood of a bygone era. Breakfast, lunch and dinner served daily; reservations necessary for both meals and overnight accommodations. Tristram C. Gaillard is the manager. The Mayflower Inn is on State Highway 47 in the village of Washington, Connecticut.

## VEAL CUTLET À LA FRANCAISE

8 veal cutlets, 1 oz. each    3 tbsp. flour
1 tsp. salt    2 whole eggs, beaten
2 oz. butter    1 cup Chablis
1 whole lemon

Pound veal with mallet. Dip in flour mixed with salt, then in eggs. Heat butter in a medium-hot pan, gently sauté cutlets in butter until they loosen from the pan and turn a light golden color. Add wine and a few slices of lemon, cover pan and simmer for 5 minutes. Arrange veal on plate, placing a slice of fresh lemon between each cutlet. Pour sauce from pan over veal and sprinkle with chopped parsley. Serves 2.

## FROZEN VANILLA SOUFFLÉ

4 egg yolks    1 cup sugar
⅛ tsp. salt    1 cup milk
1½ tsp. vanilla    1 cup light cream
2 cups whipping cream
Shaved sweet chocolate, for garnish

Beat egg yolks over hot water in double boiler; slowly add sugar, salt and ¼ cup of the milk. Add vanilla to remaining milk and light cream. Heat milk mixture, pour into egg mixture and cook slowly, stirring constantly, until lemon-colored and thick. Cool. Whip whipping cream and fold into cooled egg mixture. Pour into 1-quart soufflé dish with 3-inch paper rim. Freeze 6 to 8 hours. Garnish with chocolate shavings. Makes 6 to 8 servings.

Top: The Weather Vane, Hamden, Connecticut (painting by Don Whitney); left: The Yankee Silversmith, Wallingford, Connecticut (painting by Arthur Barbour); below: The Mayflower Inn, Washington, Connecticut (painting by George Guzzi)

**CONNECTICUT** **11**

# Homewood Inn

This comfortable and informal resort on Casco Bay in Yarmouth, Maine, was once (1742) the homestead of a sea-going family. Breakfast, lunch and dinner served every day; reservations advisable for overnight accommodations and meals. Open June 1 to mid-October. Take Exit 9 from I-95 to U.S. 1, turn right on Tuttle Road to State Highway 88, then follow signs.

## BLUEBERRY TORTE

Beat 4 eggs at medium speed for about 10 minutes or until they are lemon-colored. Gradually add 1 cup sugar. Combine 1 tsp. vanilla with ½ cup water and add. Sift the following together into batter: 1½ cups sifted all-purpose flour, 1½ tsp. baking powder and ⅛ tsp. salt. Line six 9-inch layer cake pans with waxed paper; grease and flour. Divide batter into pans; sprinkle 2 cups of blueberries over the tops. Bake at 375° for 12 to 15 minutes.

*Filling:* Whip 1 pint whipping cream until thick, adding ¼ cup confectioners' sugar. Add ¼ cup Drambuie or sherry (or 1 tsp. of vanilla). Spread cream between cooled layers, blueberry side up. Ice top layer or sprinkle with confectioners' sugar. Refrigerate before serving.

# Five Châteaux

A wall of glass at the end of the dining room affords diners a panoramic view of the Charles River and the Boston skyline here. It is in the Sonesta Hotel at 5 Cambridge Parkway, Cambridge, Massachusetts. Open daily for lunch and dinner.

## BAKED LOBSTER FIVE CHÂTEAUX

*Stuffing:* Mix together: 2 cups cracker crumbs; 4 cups bread crumbs; 2½ oz. chopped walnuts; 2 cloves garlic, crushed; ¾ cup finely chopped onion; 1 tsp. paprika; pinch each of cayenne pepper, Ac'cent (MSG) and thyme, and ¼ cup chopped parsley. Blend into this 1 cup melted butter, ½ cup clam juice, and ½ cup sherry.

Prepare six 1½-lb. live lobsters for cooking. Split them down the center of underside. Remove black sac. Place some stuffing along bottom, cover lobster with the rest. Bake at 400° for 25 minutes. Serves 6.

# Chatham Wayside Inn

On quiet, tree-lined Main Street in Chatham, Massachusetts, this hospitable old inn offers breakfast, lunch and dinner daily, year around.

## VEAL SCALLOPINI

Have the butcher cut 1½-lb. cutlets, ⅜-inch thick, from leg of veal. Pound thin with kitchen mallet. Dip pieces in flour. Heat together 1 oz. each of clarified butter and olive oil. Sauté cutlets until brown on both sides. In a separate pan sauté 12 sliced mushrooms in 1 tbsp. butter. While cutlets are cooking, lightly season with garlic salt, onion salt, Ac'cent (MSG), white pepper and celery salt.

Remove cutlets to warm platter. Add mushrooms to veal pan, then pour in 2 oz. Marsala wine and 2 oz. tomato sauce.

Turn heat up high and scrape all meat drippings from bottom of pan, stir well then pour over warm cutlets. Top with chopped parsley. Heat thin, cooked spaghetti in meat pan, add seasoned tomato sauce, top with grated Parmesan and serve.

# Captain William's House

Within easy driving distance of Cape Cod National Seashore, this charming summer restaurant is in a Colonial house on Depot Street in Dennis Port, Massachusetts. Open daily at 5 p.m., for dinner only. Reservations necessary. Open from mid-June to the last week in September.

## FILLETS OF SOLE WITH WINE SAUCE

| | |
|---|---|
| 4 fillets of sole | 1 tsp. grated onion |
| ½ tsp. salt | ¼ tsp. white pepper |
| ¼ tsp. celery salt | Dash of nutmeg |
| ½ cup white wine | 1 tsp. butter |
| ½ cup heavy cream | Worcestershire Sauce |
| | 1 tsp. cornstarch |

Place fillets on top of grated onions in ovenware serving dish. Sprinkle with salt, pepper, celery salt and nutmeg. Add wine. Dot with butter. Bake covered in moderate oven for 10 minutes. Drain off liquor, strain and add additional wine to make ½ cup. Add cream and a few drops of Worcestershire Sauce.

Bring to boil and thicken with cornstarch. Pour sauce over fillets. Garnish with blanched slivered almonds, grated carrots or parsley. Serves 4.

Top left: Homewood Inn, Yarmouth, Maine (painting by Lou McMurray); center left: Chatham Wayside Inn, Chatham, Massachusetts (painting by Frank Saso); left: Five Châteaux, Cambridge, Massachusetts (painting by C. Robert Perrin); above: Captain William's House, Dennis Port, Massachusetts (painting by Barbara Noah)

**MAINE/MASSACHUSETTS 13**

# Bill's Restaurant

Out-of-town skiers, nearby residents, and vacationing families from throughout the country frequent Bill's Restaurant, widely known for its comfortable atmosphere and first-rate food at modest prices. Broiled lobsters are a specialty. It's at 30 Federal Street in Greenfield, Massachusetts, just off I-91. Lunch and dinner served daily 11 a.m. to 11 p.m. Closed on Monday.

### BILL'S LOBSTER PIE

Blend 4 tbsp. butter with 4 tbsp. flour in saucepan over low heat. When well mixed, add 2 cups hot milk and 2 cups hot cream and cook gently for 15 minutes, stirring often. Strain and set aside. Sauté 1 lb. cooked lobster meat in 4 tbsp. butter, then add ¼ cup sherry and ½ tsp. paprika and cook another 3 minutes. Add pinch of cayenne pepper, 1 tsp. salt and cream sauce.

Beat 4 egg yolks and blend with 4 tbsp. of the sauce, then stir mixture back into lobster and remaining sauce. Cook over low heat, stirring constantly until Newburg bubbles and thickens. Remove from heat and add ¼ cup sherry. Spoon into 4 casseroles, distributing lobster meat equally. Spread with topping (below) ¼-inch thick; brown in 400° oven or under broiler. Serves 4.

*Topping:* Combine ¾ cup grated fresh bread crumbs, ¾ tsp. paprika, 3 tbsp. crushed potato chips, 1 tbsp. Parmesan cheese and 5 tbsp. melted butter.

# Flanders Motor Inn

Nestled at the base of Mt. Whittier (where John Greenleaf Whittier did much of his writing) this inn is a friendly, family-operated vacation resort in West Ossipee, New Hampshire. It is surrounded by lake and mountain recreation areas. From November through June the dining room is closed on Mondays. Reservations advisable for both meals and rooms. Charles Flanders is the owner.

### SPARERIBS WITH BARBECUE SAUCE

| | |
|---|---|
| 5 lb. spareribs | 1 cup butter |
| 1 cup minced onions | 1 tbsp. dry mustard |
| ½ cup vinegar | 1 tbsp. salt |
| 1 tbsp. horseradish | 1 tsp. pepper |
| ½ cup brown sugar | 1 cup chili sauce |
| 1 tsp. grated garlic | 1 cup tomato purée |
| 2 tbsp. Worcestershire Sauce | |

Simmer onions in butter 5 minutes. Add rest of ingredients except spareribs and simmer 10 minutes longer. Braise spareribs in hot oven until fat is removed. Dip each piece in hot sauce and bake one hour at 350°. Serves 10.

# Wolfeboro Inn

Dining in a comfortable, relaxed milieu awaits patrons at the Wolfeboro Inn, located in the oldest summer resort area in America. Overnight accommodations and recreational facilities for boating, water-skiing and swimming are available. At 44 North Main Street (State Highway 109) in Wolfeboro, New Hampshire, the inn serves breakfast, lunch and dinner daily. Closed Tuesdays from October through April.

### RHUBARB CONSERVE

Combine: 1 cup crushed pineapple, 1 cup raisins, 4 cups fresh rhubarb cut in 1-inch pieces, 4 cups sugar, and the juice and grated rind of 1 orange. Cook these ingredients over low heat, stirring frequently until thick, about 1 hour. Add ½ cup chopped nuts. Refrigerate. Use as a cold relish.

# Lydecker's

About 8 miles northwest of Paterson, on State Highway 23 in Butler, this restaurant is 15 minutes from Great Gorge and Vernon Valley ski areas. A favorite eating place in northern New Jersey for the past 25 years, it is open daily for lunch and dinner. Among specialties always on the menu are the finest clams and steamers brought in fresh daily from the North Shore and cooked to individual order. A. A. Lydecker is the owner.

### CAMEO SHRIMP

| | |
|---|---|
| 36 large raw shrimp, shelled and cleaned (about 3 lb.) | |
| ¾ cup olive oil | 3 tsp. chopped fresh garlic |
| 1½ onions, chopped | 1½ tsp. oregano |
| 1½ tsp. pepper | 1½ tsp. salt |
| ¾ cup white wine | 9 cups tomato sauce |
| Hot buttered linguini or very thin spaghetti | |

Heat oil in pan. Sauté shrimp with garlic, onion, oregano, salt and pepper until shrimp are red and onions brown. Then add wine and tomato sauce and cook for 5 minutes. Serve over hot buttered linguini or spaghetti. Serves 6.

Top left: Bill's Restaurant, Greenfield, Massachusetts (painting by C. Robert Perrin); center left: Flanders Motor Inn, West Ossipee, New Hampshire (painting by Al Albrektson); left: Wolfeboro Inn, Wolfeboro, New Hampshire (painting by Al Albrektson); above: Lydecker's, Butler, New Jersey (painting by James Krechnyak)

**MASSACHUSETTS/NEW HAMPSHIRE/NEW JERSEY** **15**

# The Lobster House

There is dockside dining at this fish house on Fisherman's Wharf in Cape May Harbor, a busy port on the New Jersey coast since whaling days. Nearby Cape May is one of the nation's oldest resorts. Open every day for breakfast, lunch and dinner. Closed on Mondays October 1 to April 1.

## CLAMS CASINO

36 cherrystone clams in shells
1 No. 2 can chopped clams
2 cloves garlic, chopped    ½ lb. butter
1 cup chopped celery    1 cup chopped onion
1 cup chopped green pepper
1 tsp. Worcestershire Sauce
1 tsp. hot sauce    1 tbsp. oregano
2½ cups bread crumbs
6 slices bacon, diced

Sauté garlic, onion, celery and green pepper (all chopped very fine) in butter. Add canned clams, Worcestershire Sauce, hot sauce, oregano and bread crumbs and cook lightly. Open raw clams and loosen meat from shell. Put 1 tbsp. hot mixture on each clam and top with raw, diced bacon. Bake in 350° oven for about 25 minutes. Makes 36 appetizers.

# Sid Allen's

This fashionable restaurant in Englewood Cliffs, New Jersey, is famous for excellent food served in elegant surroundings. It is located on U.S. 9W, a mile north of the George Washington Bridge and a short drive from Manhattan. Open every day for lunch, dinner and late evening supper. Reservations advisable. The attendant will care for your pet in a comfortable, modern kennel.

## RED SNAPPER À LA FRANCO

2 pieces red snapper (1 lb. each)
4 tbsp. olive oil    2 or 3 whole cloves
2 whole garlic cloves
2 peeled tomatoes, cut in small pieces
1 small onion, sliced thin    2 tbsp. capers
8 oz. good dry white wine
8 raw cherrystone clams
1 pinch of basil    4 slices lemon
1 pinch of sage    Chopped parsley

Coat both pieces of red snapper with flour seasoned with salt and pepper, heat both sides of fish over medium fire in deep casserole in olive oil. Then add remaining ingredients, except parsley. Cover casserole and simmer on low fire about 20 minutes. Remove garlic. Serve immediately in large soup bowls garnished with chopped parsley. Makes 4 portions.

# Zaberer's Prime Ribs Restaurant

One of the largest and best known on the East Coast, this restaurant is managed by the fourth generation of the Zaberer family. Dinner is served daily from 4 to 10 p.m.; Sunday from 2 p.m. Closed Christmas Day. Zaberer's is on Black Horse Pike near the Atlantic City race track in McKee City, New Jersey.

## ROAST DUCK WITH ORANGE SAUCE

4-lb. duck    ½ cup sugar
1 tbsp. red wine vinegar
Juice of 2 oranges    4 tbsp. lemon juice
¼ cup orange liqueur    1 grated orange rind
¼ cup orange peel, cut in thin strips

Rub cavity of cleaned duck with salt and pepper. Truss duck and prick the skin. Roast on a rack 1 hour and 40 minutes in preheated 350° oven (do not baste). Duck is done when soft if pressed. Remove excess fat from pan.

Cook sugar and vinegar in pan until caramelized. Remove from heat. Add orange juice, lemon juice, orange liqueur and grated rind; simmer. Stir until caramel has dissolved. Add to juices left in roasting pan, bring to a boil, scrape pan and stir constantly. Add orange peel and taste. Pour sauce over duck. Decorate with orange sections and parsley. Makes 4 servings.

# Tower Steak House

Bill and Elizabeth Motter founded this popular steak house, one of the state's finest. Reservations necessary for lunch and dinner which are served daily. Closed only on Christmas. It is on U.S. 22, in Mountainside, New Jersey, just minutes away from Newark.

## SAUERBRATEN

Combine 2 cups vinegar, 2 cups water, 3 bay leaves, 10 peppercorns, 1 tsp. whole cloves, 1 sliced medium-sized onion and salt and pepper to taste, and bring to boil. Pour this hot vinegar mixture over a 4-lb. pot roast, cover and marinate in refrigerator for 2 days, turning several times. Drain meat, rub with seasoned flour and brown on all sides in hot fat in a Dutch oven. Add marinade and cover tightly. Simmer for about 2½ hours.

*Gravy:* Skim any excess fat from liquid in pan, adding water if needed to make 2½ cups, and return to pan. Stir in ⅓ cup currant jelly and 8 gingersnaps, cook over low heat, stirring constantly until thick. Slice meat, cover with gravy and serve. Serves 4 to 6.

Upper left: The Lobster House, Cape May, New Jersey (painting by Max Altekruse); lower left: Sid Allen's, Englewood Cliffs, New Jersey (painting by Artemis Jegart); upper right: Zaberer's Prime Ribs Restaurant, McKee City, New Jersey (painting by Howard Whims); lower right: Tower Steak House, Mountainside, New Jersey (painting by Harvey Kidder)

# Ed Zaberer's Anglesea Inn

Since it opened in 1955, this restaurant at 400 Spruce Avenue in Wildwood, New Jersey, has been popular with patrons the year around. A special attraction is its collection of Tiffany shades, said to be the largest under one roof. Dinner served daily. Take Exit 6 from the Garden State Parkway.

### BAKED STUFFED POTATO ANGLESEA

4 large baked potatoes   ½ cup milk
4 potatoes for boiling
Salt and pepper to taste
5 tbsp. butter
8 oz. soft sharp Cheddar cheese

While baked potatoes are hot, cut in half, scooping the insides of the 4 potatoes into mixing bowl and keeping the 8 potato shells. Boil the remaining potatoes and add these to the bowl, then add milk and butter and beat until smooth. Add salt, pepper, and cut-up Cheddar cheese and continue beating until thoroughly mixed. Empty contents into a pastry bag and refill potato shells. Bake in 400° oven for 20 minutes, then place under broiler until browned. Serves 8.

# Frank Longo's Steak House

About 16 miles north of New York City, in the area of Nyack, this popular restaurant in a home (circa 1740) is located at 560 Bradley Parkway, off State Highway 303, in Blauvelt, New York. (Take Exit 5 from the Palisades Parkway or Exit 12 from the New York Thruway.) Dinner served every day except Monday. Reservations available during the week but not on weekends. Open Sunday 3 p.m. to 9 p.m. Closed New Year's Eve.

### BAKED VIRGINIA HAM

12-lb. semiboneless cooked or canned ham
Whole cloves     20-oz. can pineapple rings
1 lb. dark brown sugar     ¼ cup white vinegar
2 oz. Grand Marnier     Maraschino cherries

Place ham in roasting pan and bake at 350° until lightly brown. Remove from oven, score ham in diamond shapes, place whole clove in the corner of each diamond. Drain juice from pineapple rings in saucepan. Add brown sugar and vinegar and heat over medium fire until thickened. Add Grand Marnier. Remove from heat, pour over ham. Arrange pineapple rings on top and place a cherry in each ring. Use toothpicks if necessary to hold rings. Replace in 350° oven for 30 minutes, basting every 10 minutes. Serve hot or cold.

# Athenaeum Hotel

A landmark owned by the Chautauqua Institution, a long-established summer cultural center, the Athenaeum Hotel is one of the few operating inns of Victorian architecture remaining in the United States. It is in Chautauqua, New York, just 10 miles from Westfield. Take Exit 60 from the New York Thruway, then State Highways 17 and 17J. Open from July 1 to September 1. Breakfast, lunch and dinner daily. Reservations necessary. Overnight accommodations, vacation facilities and summer school courses available. For information write to James R. Bussey, Jr., manager.

### CREAM OF CHICKEN SOUP, LORRAINE

2 tbsp. chopped onion     1 quart chicken stock
2 tbsp. chopped green pepper
1 tbsp. chicken base
2 tbsp. chopped celery
1½ cups diced cooked chicken
1 tbsp. butter     4 oz. evaporated milk

Sauté onion, green pepper and celery in butter until soft but not brown. Add chicken stock combined with chicken base. Bring to a slow boil for 30 minutes. Make a smooth paste of 1 tbsp. cornstarch and 2 tbsp. flour in 4 oz. of water, add to chicken stock. Simmer for 5 minutes, remove from heat, add diced chicken and evaporated milk. Do not boil but let chicken get warm in hot mixture and serve. Makes 6 portions.

### CURRIE OF LAMB À LA INDIENNE

2 cups diced cooked lamb
2 tbsp. diced onion     4 tbsp. butter
¼ tsp. curry powder
2 tbsp. raisins     1 pint chicken stock
2 tbsp. flour     3 cups cooked rice
4 tsp. toasted coconut flakes

Sauté lamb cubes and onion together in 2 tbsp. butter and curry powder for 10 minutes. Add raisins and chicken stock and bring to a boil, simmer for 30 minutes. Make a roux with flour and 2 tbsp. butter and add slowly to simmering mixture. Stir gently and simmer for 4 minutes. Remove from heat. Serve lamb currie over bed of hot rice topped with sprinkling of toasted coconut flakes. Serve 4.

Top: Ed Zaberer's Anglesea Inn, Wildwood, New Jersey (painting by Howard Connolly); above: Frank Longo's Steak House, Blauvelt, New York (painting by George Samerjan); right: Athenaeum Hotel, Chautauqua, New York (painting by Hugh Laidman)

# Pierce's 1894

This restaurant was established in 1894 by the Pierce family, now in its fourth generation of management. Open Tuesday through Saturday, 4:30 to 10:30 p.m.; Sunday, 12:30 to 10 p.m. Closed on Monday and Christmas Day. The address is 228 Oakwood Avenue at 14th Street, Elmira Heights, New York.

### EGGPLANT GALATIORE

Cut 1 eggplant in half, then scoop out pulp and dice into very fine pieces. Cut 2 scallions and sauté in 3 tbsp. butter with diced eggplant. Add to this 6 oz. Alaska king crabmeat chunks and 4 heaping tbsp. cooked rice.

Season with salt, white pepper and a dash of Worcestershire Sauce. Put cooked mixture into eggplant shell, sprinkle with ¼ cup of bread crumbs and ¼ cup Parmesan cheese and dot generously with butter. Bake in 350° oven for 15 minutes. Serves 2.

# Chalet Suisse

The imaginative Swiss-born owner of this establishment, Konrad Egli, has introduced several of his own fondue creations to the American public, such as Deep Sea Fondue (below). At 6 East 48th Street in New York City; open for lunch and dinner. Closed Saturday and Sunday, holidays and for 3 weeks in August. Reservations necessary.

### DEEP SEA FONDUE CHALET SUISSE

At serving time heat fish bouillon (below) in fondue pot, keep at simmer on a chafing dish burner at table. Have ready 1 lb. fillet of sole, 12 large deep-sea scallops and 4 lobster tails, all cut into bite-size pieces. Give each diner some of each seafood and 2 forks—1 for cooking and 1 for eating—and wedges of lemon plus a variety of dunking sauces, such as hollandaise, tartar, lobster and cucumber hollandaise. Each diner cooks his own seafood, a piece at a time, in the simmering bouillon: 35 to 40 seconds for the sole, about a minute each for the scallop slices and 1½ minutes for each of the lobster segments. Serves 4 to 6.

*Fish Bouillon:* Combine 4 cups bottled clam juice; 2 cups dry white wine; 2 cups water; 1 large onion, 1 large carrot and 1 stalk celery, all chopped fine; 4 peppercorns; 1 bay leaf and ½ tsp. salt. Bring to a boil, cook over moderate heat for 30 minutes. Strain bouillon, discarding solids.

# Georges Rey Restaurant Français

This is a pleasant French restaurant with an interesting menu, a good kitchen and a medium price range. It is open daily for lunch and dinner; on Sundays and holidays it opens at 5 p.m. Reservations are necessary. At 60 West 55th Street, New York City.

### CRÊPES MAISON

To 9 tbsp. of flour add 1 tbsp. sugar and a pinch of salt. Beat in 3 eggs one at a time, then add 1 tsp. melted butter and 2 cups milk. When batter is smooth, butter a 5-inch skillet or a crêpe pan and pour a small amount of batter on the heated pan. Turn with spatula so it is cooked on both sides. Keep warm. Makes 18.

*Crabmeat Filling:* Sauté 3 chopped shallots and 1 tbsp. chopped onion in 2 tbsp. of butter. Then add 1 cup dry white wine, 1 cup tomato purée, 2 tbsp. béchamel (cream) sauce, ¾ lb. crabmeat, 1 pint whipped cream, and salt and pepper to taste. Bring to a boil and simmer. Then drop a spoonful of mixture on each crêpe and roll up around the filling.

To 1 cup béchamel sauce add ½ pint of whipping cream, whipped. Mix and pour over crêpes. Place under broiler for a minute or so until sauce is browned. Serves 6.

# Pierre Au Tunnel

This small, unpretentious restaurant in the French bistro tradition is at 306 West 48th Steet in New York City, in the heart of the theater district. Lunch, dinner and late suppers are served. Reservations necessary. Closed on Sunday.

### MOULES MARINIÈRES

Scrub 3 lb. closed mussels vigorously to make sure that sand is removed. Cut and discard the "beard." Place cleaned mussels in a large pot. Add 10 oz. water, 10 oz. dry white wine, ½ tsp. salt, 3 to 4 chives and 1 shallot (both chopped fine). Grind pepper over top, cover pot and put over high heat for about 7 minutes, or until mussels open.

Stir the mussels occasionally if they do not open immediately. After sufficient cooking time (not over 10 minutes), the mussels are ready to serve. Those that have not opened generally are not good and should not be eaten. Divide mussels and broth into 2 portions. Do not strain broth. Serves 2.

Above: Chalet Suisse, New York, New York (photo by Laszlo Studios); right: Georges Rey Restaurant Français, New York, New York (painting by Harvey Kidder); below left: Pierre Au Tunnel, New York, New York (photo by Tom Geoly); below right: Pierce's 1894, Elmira Heights, New York (painting by Ralph Avery)

# Sea Fare of the Aegean

The ancient Minoan palace of Knossos inspired the airy, columned interior of this restaurant which features the regional seafood dishes of Greece. The address is 25 West 56th Street in New York City. Open every day for lunch and dinner, noon to 11 p.m. Closed only on Thanksgiving Day. Reservations advisable.

### SHRIMP SANTORINI

Peel, devein and clean 24 jumbo shrimp, then dust lightly in flour. Sauté shrimp in 3 tbsp. butter until partly cooked and gold-colored. Place 6 shrimp in each of 4 shallow casseroles. Broil 4 tomato halves, sprinkled with oregano and Parmesan cheese, until partly cooked. Place tomato halves on top of shrimp in each casserole and top each with a slice of feta cheese. Cover with Santorini Sauce (below); bake at 400° for 5 minutes.

*Santorini Sauce:* Melt 2 oz. butter in a shallow pan; add ½ cup minced onions, 1 tsp. minced garlic, 1 tbsp. chopped fresh parsley, ¼ tsp. oregano, ¼ tsp. basil, 1 tbsp. fresh chopped dill, 2 bay leaves and 1 tsp. sugar. Bake in preheated 350° oven until golden brown. Then add 3½ cups stewed tomatoes, 1 cup ketchup and 4 cups chicken broth; continue baking for 30 minutes.

Place freshly killed 1¼-lb. lobster (or equal weight of raw unshelled shrimp) in a large saucepan. Cover lobster or shrimp with baked tomato sauce. Add 6 cups water, cover and simmer over medium heat for 1 hour, or until sauce is reduced by half. Add ½ cup sherry, 1 tsp. Maggi sauce (or Madeira wine), and salt and pepper to taste. Simmer for a few minutes more.

Remove shells from lobster or shrimp, clean and cut seafood into small pieces. Return to sauce and press all through a medium food strainer.

# The Magic Pan

Diners can watch more than 21 kinds of crepes being cooked on the magic pan wheel which rotates over a gas flame. In a charming brownstone at 149 East 57th Street in New York City, the restaurant is open from 11 a.m.

to midnight, Monday through Thursday; until 1 a.m. Friday and Saturday. Sunday, noon to 10 p.m.

### STRAWBERRY CRÊPES

*Basic Crêpe:* Beat 3 eggs well with a fork, add 1 cup unsifted flour and ⅛ tsp. salt. Beat until batter is smooth. Gradually add 1 cup milk and ¼ cup water, beating until smooth. Melt 2 tbsp. butter and set aside.

Before preparing each crêpe, brush an 8-inch crêpe pan or skillet with butter. Add batter to cover entire bottom of pan. Cook 1 minute or until lightly brown. Flip, brown lightly for about 30 seconds. Makes 12 crêpes.

*Strawberry Filling:* Mix 1 cup fresh sliced strawberries with 2 tbsp. brown sugar. Place 4 tbsp. sliced berries in the center of the crêpe. Spoon 3 tbsp. sour or whipped cream over mixture. Fold edges of crêpe over to make a roll. Garnish crêpe with 2 tbsp. sour or whipped cream and whole strawberries.

# Bus Blum's Garlock House

Gourmets from all over western New York flock to this restaurant which is housed in an 1812 mansion and is noted for fine food. In summer there is outdoor dining in an illuminated garden. It is at 401 East Main Street (State Highway 31) in Palmyra, 5 miles north of New York State Thruway Exit 43. Open for dinner every day; lunch, Monday through Friday. Overnight accommodations; reservations necessary for rooms.

### CINNAMON CARROT STICKS

8 lb. large carrots      1 quart water
2¼ cups cider vinegar
2¼ lb. granulated sugar
6 drops cassia oil (oil of cinnamon—
use eyedropper)

Slice carrots vertically into thick sticks. Cook in water until tender, not soft. Drain and place carrots in 1-gallon glass container. Mix other ingredients with 1 quart water, separately from carrots, bring to a boil and pour over carrot sticks while mix is hot. Cool before covering. Not necessary to seal. Keep under refrigeration. As carrots cool they will absorb mix. Let stand 3 to 5 days for best flavor. Carrot sticks will keep for several months under refrigeration. Delicious as an appetizer or as a relish.

Top: The Magic Pan, New York, New York (painting by G. Hyer); below left: Sea Fare of the Aegean, New York, New York, with Christopher Bastis, owner, seated, and James Tyler, head waiter (photo by Vernon Smith); below: Bus Blum's Garlock House, Palmyra, New York (painting by Diane Szaro)

**NEW YORK** **23**

# The Beeches

An Old World atmosphere pervades this year-round resort set amid 52 landscaped acres on State Highway 26, on the north side of Rome, New York. It is just 15 minutes from the New York Thruway: take Exit 32 or 33, go north to State Highway 26, by way of Turin Road to the Beeches. Breakfast, lunch and dinner served daily. Overnight accommodations and vacation facilities available. Closed Christmas Day. The Destito family owns and manages the resort.

## CHEDDAR CHEESE SOUP

½ lb. butter    1 heaping cup sifted flour
1 tbsp. paprika    4 cups milk
4 cups light cream
4 cups sharp Cheddar cheese, chopped
Salt and pepper, to taste    2 drops Tabasco
½ tsp. dry mustard, moistened
2 drops Worcestershire Sauce
Crumbled crisp bacon or chopped boiled egg

Melt butter in 2-quart heavy saucepan. When hot, add flour gradually and stir constantly for 5 minutes. Add paprika, cook over low flame and stir for 3 minutes. Combine milk and cream; add slowly to flour mixture. Do not boil. When mixture is creamy add cheese and cook slowly until cheese is melted. Add seasonings and serve in bowls topped with chopped bacon or egg. Serves 8 to 10.

# Skene Manor

Perched high up on Skene Mountain, this restaurant, housed in a historic mansion, is located half a mile north of U.S. 4 in Whitehall, New York, which is called the "birthplace of the U.S. Navy." On the inland waterway and in the vicinity of numerous lakes and mountains, the restaurant attracts sportsmen and travelers all year long. Open for dinner only; closed Tuesday except in July and August when it is open every day. Leo and "Sis" Mulholland are the owner-managers. Reservations advisable.

## BEEF STROGANOFF

Sauté 1½ cups chopped onions with 4 lb. tenderloin tips (cut in strips) in 5 tbsp. of shortening. Season to taste with salt, pepper and garlic salt. Then add 2 cups tomato soup and simmer slowly in uncovered pan for 1 hour. Add 2 cups mushrooms, heat thoroughly. When the mixture is cool add 1 cup sour cream, then reheat to serving temperature. Serve over ½ lb. buttered noodles. Makes 10 portions.

## RASPBERRY PARFAIT PIE

Drain juice from 2 cups of raspberries. Add enough water to juice to measure 1½ cups. Bring to a boil and add 1 package of raspberry gelatin and 2 cups of vanilla ice cream. If ice cream doesn't melt, beat to blend. Chill slightly, fold in raspberries and chill about ½ hour more. Pour into baked 8-inch pie shell. Top each serving with whipped cream.

*Pie Shell:*

1 cup sifted flour    ½ tsp. salt
½ cup pure lard    3 tbsp. ice water

Blend shortening with flour and salt. Add ice water. Mix until mixture holds together. Roll on floured board and bake in 450° oven until done.

## GRASSHOPPER PIE

1½ cups chocolate wafers, crumbled
½ cup melted butter    ½ cup milk
3 cups miniature marshmallows
¼ cup crème de menthe
3 tbsp. crème de cacao
2 cups whipping cream, whipped

Mix wafer crumbs and butter and press to bottom and sides of 9-inch pie pan. Bake 10 minutes at 350°. Cool. Put marshmallows and milk into saucepan. Stir constantly over very low heat for 3 minutes (until marshmallows melt). Set aside and let cool.

Add crème de menthe and crème de cacao to marshmallow mixture. Fold into whipped cream. Pour into crust. Makes one 9-inch pie. Top edges of pie with whipped cream or sprinkle with chocolate jimmies. Chill 4 hours.

ove: The Beeches,
me, New York
ainting by John
ller); right: Skene
anor, Whitehall,
w York (painting
Harvey Kidder)

# Olivos

An Italian-American cuisine distinguishes this restaurant whose owners, Philip Jannetta and Robert Jacobs, also serve as hosts. An unusual feature is the "open kitchen" which gives diners an opportunity to watch Chef Ike Eichelberger and his competent staff prepare the food. Olivos is in a residential section of Altoona, Pennsylvania, at the corner of 2nd Avenue and 1st Street. It is 10 blocks south of U.S. 220. Lunch and dinner served every day, 11 a.m. to 11 p.m., except Monday. Closed the week of the Fourth of July and Christmas Day.

### WEDDING SOUP

1½ lb. chicken backs and necks
4 quarts water      1 cup chopped celery
1 small onion, chopped fine
20 marble-sized meatballs (from your recipe)
1 head chopped endive      2 eggs
1 tbsp. grated Parmesan cheese

Boil chicken parts with water, celery and onion for 2 hours. Remove chicken from bones. Add meatballs and chicken pieces to broth and simmer 10 minutes. Add chopped endive and simmer 10 minutes more. Beat egg and add grated cheese. Pour into soup and stir. Serves 10 to 12.

# Ed's Steak House

Just a quarter mile north of Pennsylvania Turnpike Exit 11, on U.S. 220 in Bedford, Pennsylvania, this well-run restaurant is a popular stop for travelers who want good food and excellent service. Open daily 7 a.m. to 11 p.m. Closed on Christmas Day. Edward McDevitt is the owner.

### GARLIC TOAST

25 to 30 slices of French bread or party rye, sliced ¼ to ½-inch thick
¼ lb. butter      ½ small garlic bud
3 oz. Parmesan cheese, grated

Melt butter, press garlic in garlic press. Add garlic pulp and juice to butter. Mix and let stand. Butter *must* be kept melted. Brush garlic butter on bread with pastry brush.

Sprinkle with cheese. Brown top side of bread only under broiler and serve hot. (Any remaining garlic butter may be covered and refrigerated for later use.)

### THOUSAND ISLAND DRESSING

1 hard-boiled egg      4 oz. pimentos
½ green pepper      1 pint salad dressing
2 tbsp. sweet relish      ½ cup chili sauce
¾ cup ketchup

Chop egg, pimentos and pepper very fine. Add salad dressing and relish. Mix well. Add chili sauce and ketchup. Mix well. Chill and serve. Store remainder in tightly sealed jar in refrigerator.

# Fagleysville Country Hotel

This century-old hotel overlooks rolling farmlands on Swamp Pike at Sanatoga Road in Gilbertsville, Pennsylvania, which is 4 to 5 miles east of Boyertown.

All of the food served in the hotel dining room is cooked to order. Open Tuesday through Saturday for dinner from 5:30 p.m. to 9 p.m. Sunday dinner from 4 p.m. Closed on Monday. Reservations advisable. Jack Gleason is the owner.

### CHICKEN LIVER AND SMOKY CHEESE OMELET

For an individual serving, sauté 2 to 3 whole chicken livers very gently in 1 tbsp. butter, cutting the livers into small chunks with 2 knives. Remove from heat while slightly pink. *Do not overcook.* Sprinkle lightly with salt. Season 2 eggs with salt and pepper, to taste, then beat with 2 tbsp. cream.

Pour eggs into a hot skillet containing melted butter. Keep heat low until eggs are partially set. On half of the eggs sprinkle the chicken livers, 2 scallions (cut up) and 3 tbsp. smoky cheese cut in bits. Fold other half of omelet over filling and place pan in 375° oven until the eggs are set and cheese is melted, about 3 to 5 minutes.

### BEETS AND PRUNES

Cut 3 cups of canned beets into strips. Place beets and liquid in a pan with 1 lb. prunes. Season with ½ tsp. salt, 4 tbsp. sugar and 2 tsp. vinegar. Mix well, cover and steam over low heat until prunes are just done. Serve hot.

Left: Olivos, Altoona, Pennsylvania (painting by Mike Mikos); lower left: Ed's Steak House, Bedford, Pennsylvania (painting by Will Slocum); below: Fagleysville Country Hotel, Gilbertsville, Pennsylvania (painting by Ben Eisenstat)

**PENNSYLVANIA** **27**

# Lombardo's Gaslight Restaurant

Joseph Lombardo is the genial host at this restaurant, which features French-Italian cuisine. In Harrisburg, Pennsylvania, it is at 1310 North 7th Street, just north of U.S. 22. Take Pennsylvania Turnpike Exit 19, then I-83 into the city. Open for lunch and dinner every weekday until 10 p.m. Reservations necessary. Closed Sunday. Also, December 24 to 27 and July 4 to 8.

## CHAMPAGNE CHICKEN

| | |
|---|---|
| 4 boned chicken breasts | 1 cup chicken stock |
| 3 cups champagne | 3 cups whipping cream |
| 4 tbsp. chopped shallots | 8 pats butter |
| 8 oz. hot buttered noodles | |

Bone and skin chicken breasts; place in skillet, add chicken stock and cover with champagne. Add butter and shallots; cover and simmer until chicken is firm to touch—approximately 10 minutes. In a separate pan, heat cream. Season with salt and pepper. Pour over chicken in skillet and continue to simmer until thickened. Serve with buttered noodles on the side. Serves 4.

# Ben Gross Famous Restaurant

Noted for offering the finest in cuisine since 1934, this restaurant provides elegant and varied menus for lunch and dinner in two dining rooms—one styled to represent the 16th-century Tudor period, the other with an equally authentic Japanese atmosphere. It is on U.S. 30 in Irwin (near Pittsburgh), 3 miles west of Pennsylvania Turnpike Exit 7. Reservations advisable; closed Sundays and holidays.

## WASSAIL BOWL PUNCH

| | |
|---|---|
| 6 small apples, peeled and cored | |
| 1 tbsp. brown sugar | 1 tsp. nutmeg |
| 1 gallon fresh apple cider (unpasteurized) | |
| 2 tsp. cinnamon | 1 cup white sugar |
| 1 quart dry sherry | 4 thin lemon slices |

Slice apples, place in a shallow pan and sprinkle with brown sugar. Cover and bake about 20 minutes at 325°. Set aside. Bring cider to a boil and then add all remaining ingredients, stirring until sugar is dissolved. Then add apple slices and pour hot into a punch bowl. Makes thirty 5-oz. portions.

# Hotel Fauchère

Five generations of the Fauchère family have made this little hotel famous for fine food. When Louis Fauchère arrived from France in 1850, he joined the staff of the famous Delmonico's in Manhattan. He took over this hotel, 70 miles from New York City, in 1852. Overnight accommodations; all meals served daily. Reservations preferred. The address is 401 Broad Street, Milford, Pennsylvania.

## QUICHE LORRAINE

*Crust:* Line a deep 8-inch pie pan with pie crust, puff paste, or thawed frozen pie shell.

*Filling:* Fry 3 strips of bacon and 1 small sliced onion in 1 tbsp. butter until bacon is transparent. Drain and place in pie shell. Cut 2 slices Swiss cheese into matchstick strips and arrange over bacon and onion.

Beat together: 4 eggs, 2 cups thick cream and a pinch of salt. Pour egg mixture into pie shell and dot with butter (2 tbsp. in all). Bake at 375° for 30 to 35 minutes or until filling puffs high and golden.

# Hickory Bridge Farm

Family-style dinners are served in a century-old barn converted to a dining room. A hay-ride and a trip around the old-fashioned, 150-acre farm near Orrtanna, Pennsylvania, are included in the price of the meal. Farm cottages for overnight or vacations. It is a 15-minute ride from Gettysburg; go west from Lincoln Square on State Highway 116, turn right towards Orrtanna for 2 miles, then turn left on Jack Road. Meals served from noon to 8:30 p.m. Reservations advisable for meals and overnight accommodations. Closed December 23 through December 31.

## DUTCH MEAT LOAF

Mix together: 2½ lb. ground beef; 2½ cups day-old bread crumbs; 1 cup small Cheddar cheese cubes; 2 tsp. salt and ½ tsp. pepper; ½ green pepper, chopped; 1 onion, chopped; and 2 eggs. Form mixture into 2 loaves.

Put in ungreased loaf pans. Pour 1 cup ketchup over loaves and bake at 350° until done, about 1 hour. Serves 6 to 8.

Top: Lombardo's Gaslight Restaurant, Harrisburg, Pennsylvania (illustration by Thomas Schenk); left: Ben Gross Famous Restaurant, Irwin, Pennsylvania (painting by Ben Eisenstat); lower left: Hickory Bridge Farm, Orrtanna, Pennsylvania (painting by Ray Naylor); below: Hotel Fauchère, Milford, Pennsylvania (painting by Ben Eisenstat)

# Le Mont

Diners at this Pittsburgh restaurant, atop Mt. Washington, enjoy a breathtaking view of the city's Golden Triangle, where the Allegheny and Monongahela rivers meet to form the Ohio River. Open for lunch and dinner from 11 a.m. to 1 a.m. Closed Sundays and holidays. Reservations necessary. James Blandi is the manager.

## BREAST OF CHICKEN SAUTÉ MIRAMAR

Remove skin and bones from 4 halved chicken breasts then flatten. Slightly beat 3 eggs and add 3 oz. milk and a pinch of salt. Flour chicken. Dip in egg-and-milk mixture, then in bread crumb mixture (below).

Fry in 2 oz. butter and 2 oz. shortening in very hot skillet. Brown one side of chicken breast, turn, and place immediately in 400° oven. Bake 10 minutes. Remove from oven and top each chicken breast with slice of ham and Swiss cheese. Return to oven and bake for 2 minutes. Serves 4.

*Bread Crumbs and Cheese:* Store loaf of bread in refrigerator for 7 days. Cut off crust and crumble bread. Mix bread crumbs with 2 cups of Parmesan cheese, 1 clove crushed garlic, pinch of chopped parsley, ½ tsp. salt and a pinch of thyme.

# Stokesay Castle

This exact reproduction of England's Stokesay Castle is the setting for gracious wining and dining in the European manner. Overnight accommodations are also available at the Castle. Open all year for lunch and dinner; Monday through Thursday from noon until 10 p.m., Friday and Saturday from noon until 11 p.m. and Sundays from noon until 9 p.m. Sunday Feast from noon until 6 p.m. The Castle is at Hill Road and Spook Lane in Reading, Pennsylvania; take first right after Arner's Restaurant on U.S. 422; go up Glen Road to Hill Road and turn right on Spook Lane.

## GEORGIA PECAN PIE

| | |
|---|---|
| ⅔ cup pecan halves | ⅓ tsp. salt |
| 1 scant cup brown sugar | 1 tsp. vanilla |
| 1 tbsp. butter | 3 whole eggs |
| 1 cup dark Karo syrup | |
| 9-inch unbaked pie shell | |

Mix all ingredients except pecans. Place pecans in pie shell. Pour mix of remaining ingredients over pecans. Bake in 300° oven for 1 hour or until pie filling does not adhere to knife inserted into it.

# Oakhurst Tea Room

A delightful spot for travelers to stop, this 30-year-old family-operated eating place is conveniently located 6 miles west of Somerset, Pennsylvania, on State Highway 31, which runs parallel to the Pennsylvania Turnpike (Somerset is at Exit 10). Open daily, noon to 11 p.m.; smorgasbord Tuesday through Saturday, 5 to 9 p.m.

## BREAD STUFFING BALLS

| | |
|---|---|
| 2 cups chicken stock | |
| 22 oz. stale white bread, cubed | 3 eggs |
| ¼ cup chopped parsley | 1½ tsp. salt |
| ½ cup chopped green pepper | ½ tsp. pepper |
| ½ cup chopped onion | ½ cup chopped celery |
| ⅓ cup lightly browned, melted butter | |

Mix one cup of the stock into other ingredients; form into loose 2-inch balls. Arrange on pan and add remaining chicken stock. Bake in 350° oven for 15 minutes or until lightly browned. Serves 4 to 5.

## COLESLAW DRESSING

| | |
|---|---|
| 1 pint sweet cream | ½ cup vinegar |
| ½ cup sugar | 1½ tsp. salt |

Combine ingredients and whip at medium speed, about 6 minutes, until thick and creamy.

Above: Le Mont, Pittsburgh, Pennsylvania (painting by Lou McMurray); right: Stokesay Castle, Reading, Pennsylvania (painting by Arthur J. Barbour); below: Oakhurst Tea Room, Somerset, Pennsylvania (illustration by Bill Kaston)

# Kingstown Inn

There are 4 dining rooms to choose from at this friendly inn at 6725 Post Road (U.S. 1), North Kingstown, Rhode Island. Open for lunch and dinner every day except Monday. On Sundays a Swedish smorgasbord is served, 5 to 8:30 p.m. Reservations necessary. Closed in February.

## SWEDISH APPLE CAKE

Peel and slice 8 apples; add ½ cup sugar, 1 tsp. each of nutmeg and cinnamon, ½ cup brown sugar, and the juice of 1 lemon. Mix well.

Mix ½ lb. graham cracker crumbs with 2 cups melted butter. Arrange half of the apples on a 12-inch sheet pan, cover with half of the buttered crumbs; add one more layer of apples and crumbs. Bake for 40 minutes at 350°. Cut cake into small portions and serve hot or chilled, topped with sauce (below). Serves 10 to 12.

*Vanilla Sauce:* Beat together 3 egg yolks, ½ cup sugar and 1½ tbsp. cornstarch until thick and light. Gradually add 2 cups milk, stirring constantly. Cook in double boiler, stirring steadily until the mixture is custardy. Add 1 tsp. vanilla and a few drops of lemon extract.

# The Windridge Inn

This quiet country inn on Main Street in Jeffersonville, Vermont, is operated by two artists, Alden Bryan and his wife Mary. They have refurbished this old house with taste and imagination and have furnished it with handsome antiques from the area. Despite its location in a remote mountain area, the meals are gourmet fare. Prices are moderate. Attractions nearby include trout fishing, hiking, mountain climbing, and skiing in winter. Lunch and dinner served daily, except Monday lunch. Overnight accommodations. Reservations necessary.

## BRANDY PEACHES

For each serving, place juice and two peach halves in a shallow baking pan. Add 1 tbsp. maple syrup, 1 tbsp. brown sugar and 1 tsp. melted butter. Sprinkle with cinnamon and bake at 325° for about ½ hour. Can be cooled and stored in refrigerator for about two weeks. When serving, heat and pour brandy over peaches, top with ice cream or whipped cream, as desired.

# The Country Store Restaurant

For many years Vrest Orton and his son Lyman have operated the original Country Store and Victorian Restaurant on State Highway 100 in Weston in southern Vermont. This is 22 miles northeast of Manchester and U.S. 7. During the season, June 1 to November 1, the dining rooms with their 1885 décor, the famous gold-and-mahogany antique soda fountain, and the mahogany bar room are open daily for breakfast and lunch, from 8:30 a.m. to 4 p.m. Together the restaurant and the store, with its delightful and practical merchandise, are a museum of Americana.

A second Victorian-style store, with an 1871 covered bridge and overshot water wheel, is run by the Ortons in Rockingham, Vermont, on State Highway 103, two miles west of the new Connecticut Valley Highway (I-91). Both emporiums and their merchandise are reflected in the twice-yearly publication "Voice of the Mountain" which is available on request for 25 cents.

## STONE-GROUND MEAL PANCAKES

2 eggs     1⅓ cups milk
2 cups Muffin Meal*     ¾ tsp. salt
3 tbsp. maple sugar or honey
5 tsp. baking powder
¼ cup melted shortening

Mix the dry ingredients. Mix the liquids. Add former to latter, slowly; do not beat. Drop by tablespoonfuls on a 350° griddle. Cook and turn until pancakes brown on both sides, then serve with butter and Vermont maple syrup. Makes 4 to 5 portions. Serve with Vermont country sausage.

*This is a mixture of stone-ground corn, wheat and rye meals sold by the Country Store and health food stores.

Top: The Country Store Restaurant, Weston, Vermont (painting by George Samerjan); center: The Windridge Inn, Jeffersonville, Vermont (painting by John Walsh); left: Kingstown Inn, North Kingstown, Rhode Island (painting by Howard Connolly)

**RHODE ISLAND/VERMONT** 33

# Southeast

This is the realm of seafood distinguished by the imaginative touch of chefs long skilled in salt-water cooking. Yet the traditional specialties remain—the hams, the pecans, and the sweet potato pies—as well as the good plain food of the highlands. As might be expected in a region known for gracious living, the desserts are dazzling, luscious and numerous. Edward Turner's Atlantic seascape is the backdrop of this arrangement of the Southeast's bounty of native foods.

35

# Michael's Holiday Inn Restaurant

There are excellent vacation facilities at this Holiday Inn in Bessemer, Alabama, just 9½ miles southwest of downtown Birmingham on U.S. 11. The restaurant is open daily 6 a.m. to 10 p.m. Closed only on Christmas Day.

### PINEAPPLE CHEESE PIE

1 lb. cream cheese      3 oz. butter
½ cup sugar      Pinch of salt      1 tbsp. vanilla
2 oz. whole sweet milk      2 eggs, beaten
2 cups pineapple pie filling
9-inch unbaked pie shell
½ cup chopped almonds

Cream together cream cheese, butter and sugar. Add salt, vanilla, milk and eggs. Put pineapple pie filling into unbaked pastry shell. Top with cheese mixture. Sprinkle with almonds and bake in 350° oven about 40 minutes.

# Dale's Cellar Restaurant

Considered one of the best eating places in Alabama, Dale's Cellar Restaurant is at 607 North 21st Street in downtown Birmingham. Lunch and dinner served every day except Sunday.

### BEEF TIPS CREOLE

3 lb. beef sirloin tips      3 tbsp. shortening
½ cup minced onions      ¼ cup diced celery
¼ cup diced green pepper
2 tsp. Creole seasoning      ½ tsp. sweet basil
1 tbsp. minced parsley      ½ tsp. oregano
¼ tsp. chili powder      Dash of nutmeg
¼ tsp. garlic powder      ¼ tsp. salt
1 No. 2 can tomatoes      1 cup water

Cut beef tips into 1-inch cubes. Brown beef in shortening. Add vegetables, except tomatoes. Cook over medium fire for 20 minutes; stir occasionally. Add seasonings and cook 15 minutes more. Then add tomatoes and water and simmer for about 1 hour or until meat is tender. Serves 8.

# Embers Room, Holiday Inn

Fresh vegetables served with home-baked rolls and pastries have made this one of the top-rated Holiday Inn restaurants. Located on a river in Eufaula, Alabama, it has a swimming pool and offers boating, hunting, golfing and water-skiing nearby. On U.S. 82 (Riverside Drive) just 4 blocks south of U.S. 431. Open 6 a.m. to 10 p.m. every day.

### LITTLE ANN'S PEANUT PIE

2 eggs      1 cup sugar
1 stick margarine, melted
¾ cup chopped roasted and salted peanuts
¼ cup white or dark raisins      ¼ cup coconut
¼ tsp. vinegar      1 tsp. vanilla
9-inch unbaked pie shell

Beat eggs, add sugar, then margarine, then remaining ingredients. Bake in uncooked pie shell in 350° oven for 30 to 35 minutes or until pie sets.

*Pie Crust:* Mix 1 cup flour, 2 tsp. baking powder and a pinch of salt, then sift together. Add 1 tbsp. shortening and cut in with knife. Add about 3 tbsp. cold water gradually, enough to hold dough together. Knead lightly. Roll out ⅛ inch thick; place in 9-inch pie pan.

# Malaga Inn

Two graceful antebellum town houses were restored to create this restaurant which surrounds a courtyard. It is at 359 Church Street, 3 minutes from downtown Mobile, Alabama. Breakfast, lunch and dinner served daily except Sunday.

### SEAFOOD GUMBO

3 tbsp. oil or butter      2 large onions, chopped
4 stalks celery, chopped
1 large green pepper, chopped
1 lb. okra, sliced round
2 No. 2½ cans tomatoes
1 No. 2 can tomato sauce      3 quarts water
Salt and pepper to taste
Tabasco Sauce to taste
2 lb. cleaned raw shrimp      1 lb. crabmeat
1 pint raw oysters
Steamed rice

Sauté onions, green pepper and celery in oil until almost brown. Add okra, cook until tender and brown. In a large soup pot combine tomatoes, tomato sauce, water and seasonings; cook slowly for 30 minutes. Add sautéed vegetables to tomato mixture and cook for 2 hours over low heat. Add raw shrimp and cook 30 minutes, then add crabmeat and oysters and cook for 15 minutes. Serve over steamed rice. Makes 8 to 10 portions.

Top: Michael's Holiday Inn Restaurant, Bessemer, Alabama (painting by Richard Brough); above left: Dale's Cellar Restaurant, Birmingham, Alabama (painting by Richard Brough); above right: Embers Room, Holiday Inn, Eufaula, Alabama (illustration by Lou McMurray); right: Malaga Inn, Mobile, Alabama (painting by Kent Barton)

# Blue Coat Inn

Overlooking Silver Lake at 800 North State Street, this restaurant in Dover, Delaware, is owned and managed by John Koutoufaris and Roger Keith. They are famous for their excellent seafood and hearty meat dishes. Open Tuesday through Friday for lunch and dinner; Saturday dinner 5 to 10:30 p.m.; Sunday dinner noon to 9 p.m. Closed Mondays and the second full week in July. Reservations advisable.

## DELAWARE PEACH CRISP À LA MODE

Heat peach syrup from a No. 2½ can of sliced cling peaches. Mix together: 2 tbsp. cornstarch, ¼ tsp. nutmeg, ½ tsp. cinnamon, 1 cup brown sugar and 2 tbsp. honey. Blend well. Add to peach syrup. Cook until clear and thick, stirring constantly. Then add juice of 2 lemons, ½ cup raisins, ½ cup pecans and 3 cups sliced cling peaches and stir well.

Pour into deep baking dish. Make crumb topping by combining ½ cup melted butter, 1 cup flour and ½ cup white sugar. Sprinkle topping onto peach mixture. Bake for 30 minutes at 350°. Cool. Serve topped with vanilla ice cream. Makes 6 portions.

# Village Inn

This place is famous for its excellent seafood. It is in Little Creek, Delaware, on State Highway 9 (South Little Creek Road), 3 miles east of Dover by way of U.S. 13. Open daily except Monday for lunch and dinner; Sunday, noon to 9:30 p.m.

## DEVILED CLAMS

2 pints clams, minced        1 cup clam juice
¼ cup Worcestershire Sauce
1 cup combined sautéed peppers and onions
1½ tbsp. mustard
3 heaping tbsp. mayonnaise
3 dashes Tabasco Sauce
4 small eggs or 2 large eggs
Bread crumbs, to thicken

Combine ingredients except bread crumbs and mix until smooth. Add bread crumbs until mixture thickens. Pack into 50 medium-sized clam shells, dust tops with bread crumbs. Deep-fry in a basket, or bake in 400° oven for 10 minutes. Serves 10.

# The Wayside Inn

Since 1925 this restaurant has been noted for its seafood dishes, salads and homemade baked goods. Open every day except Monday for lunch and dinner, it is located in Smyrna, Delaware, on U.S. 13 at Mount Vernon Street.

## SWEET POTATO CUSTARD PIE

2 cups mashed sweet potato        2 cups milk
3 eggs        1 cup sugar        Juice of 1 lemon
Pinch of salt        1 tsp. nutmeg
Pumpkin pie spice (optional)
9-inch unbaked pastry shell

Combine all ingredients in order listed and pour into pastry shell. Bake at 350° for 40 minutes.

# Paul Young's

It's a rare day that the guest list here doesn't include a cabinet member and a few congressmen as well as visiting governors and other celebrities. Mingled with them are tourists and others who enjoy superb food and fine wines. The Young brothers, David and Paul, are the owners, managers and hosts. Open for lunch and dinner every day except Sunday. Reservations necessary. The address is 1120 Connecticut Avenue, N.W., Washington, D.C.

## LANGOUSTINE VÉNITIENNE

Sauté 16 cucumber slices (⅛ inch thick) in 2 tbsp. olive oil until soft and slightly brown. Line each of 4 coquille shells (4 to 5 inches in diameter) with 4 cucumber slices and set aside to keep warm.

Add 1 tbsp. of olive oil to the cucumber pan and sauté 16 scampi in it for 2 to 3 minutes. Remove from fire. Add a pinch of garlic powder, ¼ cup white wine and 1 cup heavy cream. Add salt to taste and return to low flame for 5 to 6 minutes. Do not boil.

Before serving add 1 tbsp. freshly chopped parsley and stir gently. Place scampi on cucumbers and cover with sauce. Serves 4.

Top: The Wayside Inn, Smyrna, Delaware (painting by Ben Eisenstat); left: Blue Coat Inn, Dover, Delaware (painting by Frank Saso); lower left: Village Inn, Little Creek, Delaware (illustration by Robert Taylor); below: Paul Young's, Washington, D. C. (painting by Max Altekruse)

# Kapok Tree Inn

Amid a setting of tropical gardens the Kapok Tree Inn in Clearwater, Florida, offers diners excellent service and good food. Open for dinner weekdays 5 p.m. to 10 p.m.; Sunday from noon to 9 p.m. The address is North Haines Road. From U.S. 19 go east on State Highway 60 to State Road 593, then north one mile.

### COLESLAW

Blend together: 1 cup thick sour cream, 1 tsp. dry prepared mustard, 1 tsp. salt, 4 tbsp. sugar, ¼ cup vinegar and 1 tsp. celery seed. Mix thoroughly. Combine with 4 cups finely cut cabbage.

# Le Dôme of The Four Seasons

Superb French haute cuisine served in a sophisticated yet congenial manner is the hallmark of this well-known restaurant in Fort Lauderdale, Florida. Patrons enjoy a rooftop view of the city and the Atlantic Ocean. Reservations suggested. Dinner from 5:30 p.m. to 11 p.m., in fall and winter; 6 p.m. to 11 p.m. in summer. The restaurant is in the penthouse of the Four Seasons Apartments at 333 Sunset Drive.

### LA TRUITE FARCIE

4 8-oz. boneless trout with skin
1 green onion, chopped fine      6 tbsp. butter
2 cups cooked fresh crabmeat
2 cups half-and-half cream
1 cup crushed saltines      2 egg yolks
Salt and pepper to taste
½ cup grated Swiss cheese

Sauté onion lightly in 1 tbsp. butter. Add crabmeat and cream. Simmer for 3 minutes. Add crushed saltines, lightly beaten egg yolks, salt and pepper. Mix well. Cook until mixture is heated through.

Sauté trout in remaining butter until lightly browned. Salt and pepper to taste. Place on ovenproof serving dish. Pour warm crab mixture over trout. Sprinkle with grated Swiss cheese. Broil until cheese is melted and browned. Serves 4.

# Mai Kai

An authentic Polynesian setting houses 7 different dining areas surrounded by magnificent gardens at this restaurant at 3599 North Federal Highway (U.S. 1) in Fort Lauderdale, Florida. Reservations suggested December through May.

### CHICKEN SHANGHAI

Skin and bone 4 half chicken breasts and cut each into 6 equal triangular pieces. Marinate chicken pieces for 1 hour in a marinade of the following ingredients:

½ cup soy sauce      2 tbsp. Mirin (sweet saki)
1 tbsp. brown sugar      1 tsp. sesame oil
1 tsp. white pepper      1 clove garlic, crushed

Roll each piece in a half slice of bacon with a sprig of coriander (or Chinese parsley) in the center. Secure with a toothpick. Deep-fry at 350° in peanut oil until bacon is crisp. Serve as hors d'oeuvres with Chinese hot mustard and sweet-sour sauce. Serves 4.

# The Clipper Room

This restaurant on the penthouse floor of the Sheraton Yankee Clipper Hotel affords diners a spectacular view of the ocean as well as excellent food. It is at 1140 Seabreeze Boulevard in Fort Lauderdale, Florida. Dinner served nightly, 6:30 to 10:30 p.m. Reservations necessary.

### DOVER SOLE À LA VERONIQUE

4 whole Dover sole, dressed
Salt and pepper to taste      ½ cup water
½ cup dry white wine      5 tbsp. butter
4 tbsp. flour      2 tbsp. whipped cream
2 tbsp. hollandaise sauce
½ cup seedless white grapes, fresh or canned

Arrange fish in shallow pan and sprinkle with salt and pepper. Add water and wine and simmer gently about 10 minutes. Remove fish to serving dish and keep warm. Make a medium-thick sauce of butter, flour and liquid left from cooking sole; correct seasonings. Blend in whipped cream and hollandaise sauce. Spread over fish, garnish with grapes and place under broiler until lightly tanned. (If fresh grapes are used, simmer them 3 minutes, then drain.) Serves 4.

Top: Kapok Tree Inn, Clearwater, Florida (painting by Frank Hagel); center left: Mai Kai, Fort Lauderdale, Florida (painting by William Turner); center right: The Clipper Room, Sheraton Yankee Clipper Hotel, Fort Lauderdale, Florida (photo by Gene Hyde Associates); left: Le Dôme of the Four Seasons, Fort Lauderdale, Florida (painting by Robert Curran Smith)

# The Down Under

An antique lover's delight, this waterfront hideaway is "down under" the Oakland Park Boulevard bridge in Fort Lauderdale, Florida. Guests enjoy its many priceless antiques as well as its excellent food. The menu includes exceptional recipes from fine restaurants all over the country. Open for lunch Monday through Friday. Dinner served every night, 6 to 11 p.m. Reservations necessary.

## QUICHE MICHELLE

2 eggs      Salt and pepper      ½ tsp. nutmeg
2 oz. fresh mushrooms, sliced thin      2 oz. ham
2 oz. grated Cheddar cheese      1 cup cream
10-inch pie shell (partly baked)

Beat the eggs with salt, pepper and nutmeg. Sauté mushrooms and ham until mushrooms are cooked. Add these and the cheese to the beaten eggs and pour into a partially baked 10-inch pie shell. Pour cream over top and bake in 350° oven for 25 minutes. Serve hot.

# Carolando Motor Inn

There are four beautiful restaurants and a show bar in this new motor hotel in Kissimmee, Florida, just a few miles from Walt Disney World. Reservations advisable. The inn is just off I-4 at the U.S. 192 exit. Norton Locke is the manager.

## COCONUT MOUSSE WITH STRAWBERRY SAUCE

6 egg whites      ½ cup 10X Sugar
1 tsp. vanilla
1 cup coconut milk (or canned piña colada mix)
4 tbsp. gelatin, dissolved in tepid water
1 pint whipping cream, whipped
½ cup toasted coconut for topping

Beat egg whites, then add sugar by tablespoonfuls while beating, until meringue is in soft peaks. Gently stir in vanilla, coconut milk and dissolved gelatin. Place in refrigerator about ½ hour, then fold in whipped cream. Chill for additional 1½ hours. Top with toasted coconut and strawberry sauce (below). Can be made in 6-oz. champagne glasses. Serves 6.

*Strawberry Sauce:* Combine 10 oz. frozen strawberries, ¼ cup finely shredded coconut and 1 oz. orange-flavored liqueur. Blend well and allow to chill in refrigerator for 30 minutes.

# Lobster House

Ninety feet of windows fronting on Boca Ciega Bay provide diners with a view of the Gulf and the Madeira Beach Bridge in this attractive restaurant at 565 150th Avenue in Madeira Beach, Florida (north of St. Petersburg). Open every day, noon to 1:00 a.m. Closed Christmas Day. Eugene Mueller is the owner.

## FROG LEGS SUPRÊME

Combine 1 cup flour, ½ tsp. onion salt, ½ tsp. garlic salt and ½ tsp. celery salt. Mix well. Roll 16 pairs of frog legs in flour mixture. Combine melted butter with 2 large cloves garlic, chopped fine; ½ tsp. Ac'cent (MSG); ½ tsp. onion salt and ½ tsp. celery salt.

Fry coated frog legs in garlic butter mixture on both sides over low heat, keeping pan covered, until golden brown. Add juice of half a lemon and serve immediately. Serves 4.

# Hilton House of Beef

This restaurant boasts the finest beef in central Florida. In the evening there is dining on the patio, overlooking the inn's tropical garden and swimming pool. Open daily for breakfast, lunch and dinner. The address is 3200 West Colonial in Orlando. It is 8 miles east of Florida's Turnpike Exit 25 on West Highway 50. Overnight accommodations.

## BLUE CHEESE DRESSING

Blend together 1 oz. blue cheese, 1 oz. buttermilk, pinch of garlic powder or a few drops of garlic juice, 1 drop hot sauce and 1 drop Worcestershire Sauce. Add 1 cup mayonnaise and 1 cup sour cream and blend again. Stir in 1 oz. more of blue cheese. Serve on a tossed salad.

Upper left: Carolando Motor Inn, Kissimmee, Florida (photo by Bob Braun); lower left: Lobster House, Madeira Beach, Florida (painting by Larry Tople): upper right: The Down Under, Fort Lauderdale, Florida (painting by Robert Curran Smith); lower right: Hilton House of Beef, Orlando, Florida (painting by Robert Curran Smith)

# Skyline Restaurant

A bountiful buffet is offered every day for lunch and dinner at this fine restaurant which overlooks the Herndon Airport in Orlando, Florida. Closed on Sunday. By special reservation groups of 4 or more can order the Gourmet Dinner which features a mountain of shrimp on ice, oysters Rockefeller, fabulous stone crabs, lobster thermidor, char-broiled filet mignon plus many garnishes and salads.

### ALMOND TORTE

1 egg     1 egg yolk     ¾ cup sweet butter
1½ cups confectioners' sugar
½ cup cocoa
1 tsp. each vanilla and almond flavoring
1½ cups ground or chopped almonds
32 social tea biscuits (or any plain cookie),
broken into 6 to 8 pieces
1 pint whipped cream or
1 quart vanilla ice cream

Beat egg, egg yolk, butter, sugar, cocoa and flavorings in mixer until mixture is fluffy. Fold in almonds and cookie pieces. Spoon into oiled 1½-quart mold; refrigerate 6 hours or overnight. Unmold, invert on serving dish. Serves 12 in thin slices topped with whipped cream or ice cream.

# Willoughby's

This Orlando restaurant has become one of central Florida's most popular. Lunch and dinner served every day; reservations necessary. It is at 3911 East Colonial Drive (State Highway 50).

### MUSHROOMS EN CASSEROLE

Sauté 24 whole, fresh mushrooms using the following seasoned butter: Soften ½ lb. butter in a bowl; add 1 tbsp. chopped shallots, ½ tsp. black pepper, juice of 1 lemon, ½ tsp. salt, 1 tbsp. Worcestershire Sauce and 4 sprigs of freshly chopped parsley; blend together. Sauté mushrooms until brown, remove from pan.

Add 2 cups burgundy and 2 cups water to saucepan. Add juice of 1 lemon, ½ tsp. salt, ¼ tsp. white pepper and a pinch of rosemary leaves. When mixture comes to slow boil add ½ cup cornstarch blended with a small amount of water until desired thickness is achieved. Pour over mushrooms.

# Seven Seas

Open-hearth cooking, tempting seafood dishes and a Sunday evening smorgasbord in elegant surroundings attract diners to this restaurant in Panama City, Florida. Open daily for lunch and dinner from 11 a.m. to 10 p.m. at 18 West 5th Street.

### SHRIMP AND CRABMEAT AU GRATIN

Sauté 1 lb. lump crabmeat and 1 lb. boiled shrimp in 3 tbsp. butter. Add 2 tsp. sherry, 3 oz. American cheese and 3 cups hot, medium-thick cream sauce. Season with salt and pepper. Cook thoroughly, pour into casserole. Sprinkle top with ½ cup crushed cracker crumbs, ½ cup Romano cheese and 1 tbsp. paprika. Dot with butter and bake in 350° oven until brown. Serves 4 to 6.

# Martine's

Each of Martine's 13 rooms features a truly distinctive Old World décor. Open daily from 11:30 a.m. to 12:30 p.m.; until 1:30 a.m. Friday and Saturday; coffee shop open 24 hours every day except Christmas. The address is 4101 West Mobile Highway (U.S. 90 and 98), Pensacola, Florida.

### FABULOUS NUT CAKE

Cream ¾ lb. butter with 2 cups sugar. Add 12 egg yolks, two at a time, creaming them into mixture well. Add the grated rind and juice of 2 oranges and 1 lb. chopped pecans.

Crush 6 oz. zwieback and blend with ½ tsp. each of cinnamon, nutmeg and clove, and a pinch of salt. Combine dry ingredients with creamed mixture. Add 2 tsp. baking powder. Beat 12 egg whites until they form peaks, then fold into mixture. Pour batter into buttered 18x12x2-inch pan and bake about 40 minutes at 350°. Twenty minutes after cake is removed from oven top with warm syrup.

*Syrup:* Combine 2 cups sugar, 1 cup water and 1 tbsp. lemon juice. Bring to a boil until sugar dissolves and mixture thickens slightly. Remove from stove and add 1 tbsp. apricot liqueur. Pour over warm cake. Makes about 35 squares. Can be served warm, or chilled and topped with whipped cream.

Left: Skyline Restaurant, Orlando, Florida (painting by Robert Curran Smith); center left: Willoughby's, Orlando, Florida (painting by Robert Curran Smith); center right: Seven Seas, Panama City, Florida (painting by Robert Curran Smith); below: Martine's, Pensacola, Florida (painting by Harvey Kidder)

# Papeete Bay Verandah

There is a South Seas enchantment, as well as excellent food, in this dining room of the Polynesian Village Hotel in Walt Disney World near Orlando, Florida.

### CHICKEN LICHEE

Season 6 large boneless, skinless chicken breasts with a little salt, dip into batter (below) and deep-fry in 1 quart oil at 350° until brown and sufficiently done, about 15 minutes. Arrange on a platter, surround with lichee nuts and cover with sweet-and-sour sauce (below). Serves 6.

*Batter:* Combine 1 cup all-purpose flour, 1 tsp. Ac'cent (MSG), ¼ tsp. garlic powder, ¼ tsp. ginger, ¼ tsp. ground white pepper. Add 3 eggs and ¼ cup cold water, beat until thoroughly blended. Add about ¼ cup more water until consistency is that of a thin pancake batter. Add 1 tsp. baking powder and 1 tbsp. sesame oil; mix thoroughly. Let stand at room temperature 20 minutes.

*Sweet-and-Sour Sauce:* Combine 4 cups water, 1 cup sugar, 1¼ cups white vinegar, juice from 1 small can pineapple chunks (reserve chunks), 1 small can lichee nuts and ¼ cup soy sauce; bring to a rolling boil.

Dissolve ¼ cup cornstarch in ½ cup sauterne and add to boiling liquid, stirring constantly 3 to 4 minutes after liquid returns to boil. Sauce should be thick. Add 1 drop red and 2 drops yellow food color, stir. Add 1 cup diced onions, ½ cup diced green pepper and pineapple chunks. Cook 10 minutes more, continue stirring.

# Pittypat's Porch

Named for a character in "Gone With the Wind," this restaurant is in a replica of an antebellum mansion. Dinner served daily; closed Sunday. The address is 25 Cain Street, N. W., Atlanta.

### QUAIL WITH WILD RICE

Clean and dress 8 quail; sew body cavity together. Sauté in ¼ lb. butter until brown. Bake in covered dish at 325° for about 30 minutes. Keep basting with white wine mixed with water.

In ¼ lb. butter sauté 1½ lb. chicken livers, 2 large onions, chopped; 1 green pepper, chopped; 2 cloves garlic, minced; and 10 whole mushrooms, sliced. Do not let vegetables brown, but cook to a light golden color. Add 2½ cups cooked wild rice, 2 cups chicken broth and 1½ cups port wine. Place mixture in 3-quart baking dish, cover and bake at 325° for 20 minutes or until liquid is absorbed. Serve quail over rice. Serves 8.

# The Midnight Sun

The focal point of the elegant dining room here is a magnificent tiered marble fountain. The menu features Scandinavian dishes. It is at 235 Peachtree Street, N.E., in Peachtree Center, Atlanta. Lunch served Monday through Friday; dinner, Monday through Saturday. Reservations necessary.

### ROAST VENISON

Rub a 5- to 6-lb. saddle of venison with 2 tsp. salt and ¼ tsp. pepper and cover with thin slices of bacon. Roast at 375° until brown, about 30 minutes. Blend 4 tbsp. flour with 1 cup cold milk, then stir in 1 cup boiling milk; blend smooth. Add any meat drippings, season with salt and pepper and boil well. Pour this gravy over venison and roast at 310° for 1½ hours. Baste frequently. When meat is tender remove from oven, discard bacon.

Skim excess fat from gravy, add a little cream and simmer until desired consistency is reached. Add a pinch of sugar and a spoonful of currant jelly or tomato purée. Pour a little gravy over the roast; serve remainder separately.

# The Old Mill

This quaint restaurant is housed in an old mill constructed in 1848 with hand-hewn boards and wooden pegs. Dinner served daily from 5 to 11 p.m. Closed Christmas Day. It is 2 miles south of Cedartown, Georgia, on U.S. 27.

### CORNBREAD

Mix 2½ cups self-rising corn meal, ½ cup self-rising flour, ¼ tsp. baking soda and 1 tbsp. sugar. Add 1 slightly beaten egg and 1¼ cups buttermilk; beat well. Heat 3 tbsp. bacon drippings in 9-inch iron skillet and pour into mixture. Mix well. Pour mixture into skillet, bake in 425° oven 20 to 25 minutes until golden brown. Cut in wedges, 6 to 8 portions.

# Southeast

Left: Papeete Bay Verandah, Walt Disney World, Florida (photo by Bob Braun); lower left: Pittypat's Porch, Atlanta, Georgia (painting by James Crabb); upper right: The Midnight Sun, Atlanta, Georgia (painting by Max Altekruse); lower right: The Old Mill, Cedartown, Georgia (painting by Richard Brough)

**FLORIDA/GEORGIA** **47**

# Cag's Open Hearth

Everything is cooked to individual order at this gourmet restaurant at 4330 Forsyth Road in Macon, Georgia. Take Wesleyan College Exit from I-475 or I-75. Dinner only served every day except Sunday. Reservations preferred. Angelo Cagliostro is the owner and manager.

### NEPTUNE CASSEROLE

4 cups béchamel sauce (basic white-wine sauce)
16 cooked medium-sized shrimp
6 oz. cooked lobster meat
8 chopped mushrooms
6 oz. flaked crabmeat      Paprika

Mix sauce with seafood and mushrooms and divide mixture into four 8-oz. individual casseroles. Sprinkle with paprika. Bake in 325° oven for 30 minutes or until sauce begins to simmer. Serves 4.

# The Cloister

In the famed Golden Isles of Georgia, this year-round seaside resort is on Sea Island, just 14 miles east of I-95 over a causeway. Breakfast, lunch and dinner served daily. The painting shows the traditional Sunday night buffet. Reservations necessary for meals and overnight accommodations. I. A. Harned is the manager.

### CABBAGE SOUFFLE À LA CLOISTER

Cook 2 tbsp. finely chopped shallots or onions in ½ cup butter or bacon fat until they are transparent. Add ½ cup flour and 2 cups coffee cream. This will make a thick cream sauce.

Grind 2 lb. cooked green cabbage through a fine blade or chop fine with a knife and combine with cream sauce, adding a pinch of salt, pepper and nutmeg. Stir well, bring to a boil and remove from fire. Add 8 egg yolks 1 at a time, stirring constantly. Beat 8 egg whites until stiff and gently fold into mixture. Pour into a greased deep baking dish. Set in a pan of water and bake in 350° oven for 10 minutes. Serves 10.

# Tassey's Pier

About 8 miles from downtown Savannah, this seafood house is located in Thunderbolt, Georgia, a quaint fishing village which harbors the state's shrimp fleet. The dining room is built out over the water on the Wilmington River and specializes in freshly caught local seafood. Open for lunch and dinner, Monday through Saturday. Closed Sunday.

### TUB OF SHRIMP

Combine 1 cup white vinegar, 1 tsp. pickling spices, a pinch of cayenne pepper and 1 tsp. salt; bring to a boil. Add 1 lb. unshelled shrimp and cook covered for 2 minutes, then stir and cook for another minute. Remove from fire and let set for 3 minutes. Strain, peel and eat while hot. Serves 2 to 4.

### CRABMEAT STEW

Sauté ½ lb. crabmeat in 1 tbsp. butter until hot. Add 20 oz. milk and bring to a boil. Remove from fire and add 2 oz. sherry. Pour into 4 cups. Float a slice of lemon in each cup and sprinkle each with a dash of paprika. Serves 4.

# Ramada Imperial House

Luxury accommodations, excellent cuisine and superb service are the winning combination at this Kentucky inn which is surrounded by world-famous Thoroughbred farms. Reservations necessary for both meals and hotel accommodations. The address is 525 Waller Avenue, Lexington.

### QUICHE LORRAINE

4 eggs      ½ cup flour      4 cups milk
Salt and pepper to taste      Pinch of nutmeg
½ lb. bacon, chopped and fried crisp
¼ lb. chopped ham
2 cups shredded Gruyère cheese
10-inch unbaked pastry shell

Beat eggs until light, add flour, milk and seasonings and mix well. Pour into unbaked crust. Sprinkle bacon, ham and cheese over the custard. Bake at 380° for 25 minutes. Serves 6.

Upper left: The Cloister, Sea Island, Georgia (painting by Lou McMurray); left: Cag's Open Hearth, Macon, Georgia (painting by Adele Bichan); lower left: Tassey's Pier, Thunderbolt, Georgia (painting by Larry McManus); right: Ramada Imperial House, Lexington, Kentucky (painting by Ray Naylor)

# Casa Grisanti

Delicately seasoned Italian dishes and sauces concocted from recipes that have been in the Grisanti family for generations are served here. Lunch from 11 a.m. to 2:30 p.m.; dinner, 5 p.m. to 11 p.m. Monday through Thursday, 5 p.m. to midnight Friday and Saturday. Closed Sundays and holidays. The address is 1000 East Liberty Street, Louisville, Kentucky, 8 blocks east of I-65.

## SPAGHETTI WITH CLAM SAUCE

½ cup olive oil        2 large cloves garlic, minced
¼ cup parsley, chopped fine        ½ tsp. salt
½ tsp. pepper        1 lb. fine spaghetti, cooked
2 cans minced clams and juice (7½-oz. size)

Brown garlic lightly in the olive oil over low heat. Add clam juice (but not clams) and remaining ingredients except spaghetti, and cook over higher heat while stirring constantly. Add clams, bring to a boil. Serve over hot spaghetti. Serves 4.

# Dobbs House Luau

If you want to escape the hurly-burly of Standiford Airport (Lee Terminal) in Louisville, Kentucky, go through the door to this Shangri-la and within minutes you are being served a Polynesian feast in the exotic atmosphere of the South Seas. Open for lunch and dinner every weekday. Reservations advisable. Closed on some holidays.

## ALMOND CHICKEN

2 cups raw chicken meat
4 tbsp. oil        1 tsp. salt
⅔ cup diced bok choy or Swiss chard leaves
2 oz. water chestnuts, sliced in thin strips
2 oz. sliced mushrooms        ⅔ cup diced celery
⅔ cup diced bamboo shoots
1½ cups chicken stock
½ tsp. molasses        1 tbsp. Ac'cent (MSG)
½ tsp. sugar        2 cups hot rice
2 tbsp. cornstarch mixed with ¼ cup water
32 whole blanched almonds, sautéed in butter

Cut chicken into pieces 3/16 inch thick, ½ inch wide and 1½ inches long. Sauté lightly with oil and salt. Add vegetables and sauté for a few seconds. Add chicken stock, cover pan and steam for about 2 minutes until mixture is boiling. Add molasses, Ac'cent and sugar, mixing well. Add cornstarch and water mixture, just enough to thicken the sauce. Place a mound of rice in the center of each plate, surrounded with chicken mixture. Sprinkle with almonds. Makes 4 portions.

# The Normandy Inn

This fascinating riverfront restaurant is housed in a 115-year-old building which the present owner, Paul O'Brien, restored in 1968 with taste and imagination. The address is 644 West Washington Street, Louisville, Kentucky. Open for lunch Monday through Friday; for dinner every day except Sunday. Reservations necessary.

## RED SNAPPER GRAND DUC

Poach any number of red snapper fillets until ¾ done. Place each on top of 4 to 6 spears of cooked asparagus, on a greased oven pan; cover each with at least ¼ cup hollandaise sauce. Bake in 350° oven for 15 minutes. Top each serving with a mushroom cap.

# Orchard Inn

Founded in 1935 in an apple orchard, this restaurant specializes in seafood fresh from Chesapeake Bay. Owned and operated by two brothers, Charles and James Esserwein, it is open daily for lunch and dinner. It is located in Towson, Maryland (Baltimore County). Take Beltway Exit No. 29 (Loch Raven Boulevard) to Joppa Road, turn right and go about 3 blocks to 1528 East Joppa.

## CHICKEN MARENGO

Flour a whole, disjointed chicken, then pan-fry in ¼ cup oil until fully cooked. Remove chicken and drain off all but 4 tbsp. of drippings from pan.

Add 4 tbsp. flour to the drippings and brown well. Add 1 cup whole canned tomatoes, 1 cup water, 4 tbsp. dry white wine, 10 whole cocktail olives, 1 finely chopped garlic clove, and 10 cocktail onions. Place cooked chicken in sauce and cook 20 minutes. Serve in a casserole. Serves 2.

## DEEP DISH LOBSTER

2 lb. cooked lobster meat
3 cups chopped mushrooms
3 cups mayonnaise        6 eggs
6 tsp. Worcestershire Sauce
6 tbsp. grated Parmesan cheese

Mix all ingredients together except cheese in a bowl. Put in six 8-oz. casseroles, top with cheese. Bake at 450° for 20 minutes.

Above: Casa Grisanti Louisville, Kentucky (painting by Chuck Jordano); right: Dobbs House Luau, Louisville, Kentucky (painting by Robert Boston); lower left: The Normandy Inn, Louisville, Kentucky (photo by Robert Boram); lower right: Orchard Inn, Towson, Maryland (painting by Frank Saso)

# Seafare Restaurant

A perfect ending to a day in the sun and sand and surf on North Carolina's Outer Banks is a seafood or western beef dinner in the Early American dining rooms of Seafare at Nags Head. Nearby are Cape Hatteras National Seashore and the drama, "Lost Colony," performed on Roanoke Island. Seafare is open daily from 5 p.m. to 10 p.m. from May 1 to September 30; 5 p.m. to 9 p.m. from October 1 to April 30.

### LEMON CHESS PIE

2 cups sugar     1 good pinch salt
1 tbsp. water-ground white or yellow cornmeal
1 tbsp. flour     ¼ cup melted butter
¼ cup milk     4 eggs
2 lemons (juice and grated rind)
9-inch unbaked pie shell

Combine sugar, salt, cornmeal and flour. Add melted butter (slightly cooled), milk, lemon rind and juice; and eggs; beat well. Slip the unbaked pie shell under the hot broiler for 60 seconds to improve the crust, then pour pie mixture into it. Bake at 350° for 40 minutes, center should be barely firm. Serves 6.

# Angus Barn

Known as the "Beefeater's Haven," this fine restaurant in a big red barn is on U.S. 70 between Raleigh and Durham, North Carolina. Open every evening for dinner, on weekdays from 5:30 p.m. to 11:30 p.m.; Sundays 5:30 p.m. to 10 p.m. Reservations advisable. Angus steer beef is cooked over large charcoal pits where customers can watch.

### STUFFED POTATOES

Grease 6 large Idaho potatoes and bake them at 400° for 45 minutes. Cut in half lengthwise. Spoon out centers while hot (save skins) and put into mixing bowl.

*Stuffing:* Combine 1 tsp. salt, 1tbsp. chives (chopped), 2 tbsp. crumbled cooked bacon, 4 oz. butter or margarine, 3½ tbsp. grated Parmesan cheese, ½ tsp. black pepper, ⅛ tsp. Ac'cent (MSG) and 1 tbsp. sour cream.

Combine this mixture with spooned-out centers of potatoes and mix with electric mixer for 3 minutes at medium speed. Spoon

into potato skins; sprinkle lightly with paprika. Brown in hot oven about 4 minutes. Serves 8 to 12.

# Ziggy's Restaurant

For over a quarter of a century the F. R. Hartzog family has owned and operated this popular restaurant north of Bamberg, South Carolina. Its specialty is quality Southern food, cooked to suit the taste of the Carolina low country. It opens for breakfast at 5 a.m. and serves lunch and dinner to 10 p.m. every day. Closed on Christmas Day and July 4. Reservations advisable for the Sunday noon buffet. Ziggy's is on U.S. 301, just north of its intersection with U.S. 78.

### ICE BOX LEMON MERINGUE PIE

1 can sweetened condensed milk
½ cup lemon juice     2 eggs, separated
Grated rind of 1 lemon     ¼ tsp. lemon extract
8-inch graham cracker pie shell
2 tbsp. sugar     ¼ tsp. cream of tartar

Blend milk, juice, egg yolks, grated lemon rind and lemon extract until mixture thickens. Pour into pie shell and cover with meringue, made by beating egg whites until foamy, then gradually adding sugar and cream of tartar. Bake in 350° oven until meringue is golden brown. Chill before serving.

# The Market Place

This restaurant is located in a former church in the old waterfront section of downtown Charleston, South Carolina. The address is 32 Market Place. Open daily for dinner from 6 p.m. to 10:30 p.m. Closed on Monday. Reservations necessary. Wilbur Burbage is the owner-manager.

### BLAZING BANANA

2 tsp. butter     3 tsp. dark brown sugar
1 oz. banana liqueur     1 large banana, sliced
Dash of nutmeg     3 dips vanilla ice ceam
1 tsp. flaming brandy

Place butter, sugar and liqueur in a chafing dish over low heat, mix until a paste. Add banana and nutmeg. Cook for about 5 minutes or until banana is soft. Pour over ice cream and top with flaming brandy. Makes 1 serving.

Above: Seafare Restaurant, Nags Head, North Carolina (painting by Peter Rex Denby); right: Angus Barn, Raleigh, North Carolina (painting by Joe Cox); lower left: Ziggy's Restaurant, Bamberg, South Carolina (painting by Howard Whims); lower right: The Market Place, Charleston, South Carolina (painting by Mike Mikos)

**NORTH CAROLINA/SOUTH CAROLINA** 53

# Fripp Island Inn

This South Carolina resort on the ocean offers tennis, riding, 4-season golf, fishing and swimming. It is on Fripp Island at the end of U.S. 21 (17 miles east of Beaufort). Open daily for all meals; reservations necessary.

## PINEAPPLE JUBILEE

Pare, slice and core two fresh pineapples and heat slices in skillet with ½ cup orange marmalade. Pour 1 oz. rum over pan and ignite, spooning sauce over fruit. Serve in sauce dishes containing vanilla ice cream, with fruit placed on one side of ice cream and flaming sauce spooned on other side. Serves 8 to 10.

# Martha Washington Inn

In a 12-acre park in Abingdon, Virginia, this inn is a delightful place to sample old-fashioned Southern cooking. All meals served daily; overnight accommodations. The address is 150 West Main Street. From I-81 take Exit 8.

## SCALLOPED OYSTERS AND CORN

3 cups saltine cracker crumbs
(don't use cracker meal)
½ cup melted butter
4 cups cream-style corn mixed with ½ cup cream
16 oysters; drain, save ½ liquor

Combine cracker crumbs and butter. Place 1 cup of mixture in bottom of a deep 2-quart casserole. Cover with half of the corn mixture, then arrange half of the oysters over top of corn. Season oysters lightly with salt (unless salted crackers are used) and moisten with part of oyster liquor.

Now add another layer of crumbs (1 cup), another of the corn mixture, and another of oysters (also seasoned and moistened). Finish with a layer of remaining crumbs. Bake at 375° for about 40 minutes. Serves 8.

# George Washington's Old Club Restaurant

This historic eating place is at 555 South Washington Street (U.S. 1) in Alexandria, Virginia. The oldest part of this beautiful Colonial home was originally built by a company of gentlemen, among whom were George Washington and George Mason. It was used as a clubhouse and moved to its present location in 1790. Lunch and dinner served daily, except Mondays and Christmas.

## DEEP DISH APPLE PIE

12 medium-sized apples (about 3½ lb.)
¼ lb. butter        1 cup brown sugar
½ cup granulated sugar        1½ tsp. nutmeg
1½ tsp. cinnamon        ⅓ cup flour
½ tsp. salt        2 oz. apple wine
4 oz. apple juice
Pie crust for 8 x 12 x 2-inch pan

Peel, core and slice apples and place in deep baking pan. Cut butter into thin slices and divide evenly over apples. Blend remaining ingredients except crust and sprinkle over apples. Roll out pie crust about ½ inch thick and cover apples with it.

Cut eight 1-inch vents in crust. Bake at 425° for 45 minutes; lower temperature to 325° and continue baking until crust is brown and apples are cooked. Serves 8.

# The Farmhouse

This Early American restaurant is located in an old farmhouse in a pleasant rustic setting just off U.S. 460 near Christiansburg in southwestern Virginia. Meals served 4 p.m. to 11 p.m. Monday through Saturday. Closed on Sunday.

## CHOCOLATE LUSCIOUS PIE

*Graham Cracker Crust:* Combine 1½ cups graham cracker crumbs, ½ cup finely chopped pecans, ⅓ cup brown sugar and ½ cup melted butter. Pack mixture firmly onto bottom and sides of a 10-inch pie pan. Bake at 300° for 5 minutes, cool.

*Filling:* Heat 1¼ cups milk with ⅓ cup sugar. Add 2 egg yolks, cook 2 minutes, stirring constantly. Soften 1 envelope Knox gelatin in ¼ cup milk and add to hot mixture. Cool until partially set. Fold in 1 cup whipping cream, whipped, and 2 egg whites which have been beaten until stiff with ⅓ cup sugar. Cut 1 square semisweet chocolate with a vegetable peeler and add to mixture. Stir in 1 tsp. vanilla. Pour into crust, chill. When filling has set, heat ½ cup chocolate chips, ⅓ cup water and 1 tbsp. butter to make a smooth sauce. Drizzle over top of pie. Serve chilled and top with whipped cream.

Upper left: Fripp Island Inn, Fripp Island, South Carolina (painting by Harvey Kidder); lower left: George Washington's Old Club Restaurant, Alexandria, Virginia (painting by Robert Atwood); upper right: Martha Washington Inn, Abingdon, Virginia (painting by Mike Dorsey); lower right: The Farmhouse, Christiansburg, Virginia (painting by Horace Day)

**SOUTH CAROLINA/VIRGINIA**

# Wayside Inn

Since 1797 this inn has welcomed travelers who came first by foot or on horseback, then by stagecoach and later by car. Breakfast, lunch and dinner served; overnight accommodations. Located in Middletown, Virginia, about 75 miles west of Washington, D. C., on U.S. 11.

## AUNT REBEKAH'S PECAN PIE

Beat 4 eggs slightly, then add ½ cup sugar. Stir in 3 cups maple syrup, a pinch of salt and ¼ tsp. vanilla. Add 1 cup pecans. Pour into 9-inch unbaked pie shell. Bake for 10 minutes in 450° oven, then reduce to 350° and bake 30 to 35 minutes or until knife inserted in center comes out clean.

# Pine Tree Inn

This landmark Virginia restaurant is still operated by the Davis family after 44 years. It is located at 2932 Virginia Beach Boulevard in Virginia Beach. Open weekdays 5 p.m. to 10 p.m.; Sundays noon to 10 p.m.; closed Christmas Day only.

## MARINATED STRING BEANS

2 cans cut green beans (1-lb. size)
⅔ cup sugar      ⅔ tsp. salt
⅔ cup cider vinegar      ½ cup chopped onion
Pinch of black pepper      1 tbsp. salad oil

Drain beans, reserving ⅓ of juice, and discarding the remainder. Dissolve sugar and salt in juice combined with vinegar. Mix together beans, onions and black pepper, then pour on vinegar mixture. Add oil and stir gently to prevent beans from breaking. Chill overnight.

# Nick's Seafood Pavilion

One of the most charming restaurants in historic Yorktown, Virginia, Nick's specializes in seafoods, blue-ribbon steaks and unique salads. It is on Water Street near the south end of Coleman Bridge. Lunch and dinner served daily except Christmas Day. Reservations necessary.

## LOBSTER DIEN BIEN

2 lb. fresh lobster meat
6 oz. butter      ⅔ cup chopped scallions
1 green pepper, diced
1¼ cups fresh mushrooms
½ cup Uncle Ben's converted rice
3 ripe tomatoes      ⅔ cup chicken consommé
1 tsp. powdered tarragon      1 tsp. pepper

Cut lobster in small pieces, season with ½ tsp. pepper and ⅓ tsp. salt, then brown in 4 oz. of butter in pan. Partly brown lobster in butter, making sure that butter is hot enough so lobster will not lose juice. Chop scallions, pepper and mushrooms and add to lobster.

Simmer 5 minutes. Add rice, stirring continuously, until rice is loose. Add tomatoes, chopped fine, and consommé. Stir once and cover. Cook about 25 minutes, then remove from heat. Put remaining 2 oz. butter in a pan and brown evenly, then add tarragon and pepper. Pour over lobster and mix well. Serves 3.

# Greenbrier

This 90-year-old family resort is on 6,500 acres in the Allegheny Mountains in White Sulphur Springs, West Virginia. It is on U.S. 60 one mile southeast of I-64. The three dining rooms serve breakfast, lunch and dinner every day. American Plan for guests; reservations suggested for visitors. Extensive vacation facilities.

## SWISS CHEESE FONDUE

Rub an earthenware casserole with a clove of garlic. Add 2 cups Neuchâtel wine and heat slowly over chafing dish burner. Lightly mix 1 lb. shredded Gruyère cheese with ½ tsp. flour. When the bubbles in the wine rise to the surface (do not boil) add cheese mixture, a handful at a time, stirring until each handful melts. Add freshly ground pepper, salt, nutmeg and 2 tbsp. kirschwasser; stir well. Turn heat low but keep fondue slowly bubbling.

Cut 1 loaf French bread into cubes, leaving one side of crust on each. Provide long-handled forks. Each guest impales a bread cube through the crust and dunks it into the fondue, stirring it around as he does. If fondue becomes too thick, add a little hot wine (never cold). Serves 4.

Top: Wayside Inn, Middletown, Virginia (painting by Horace Day); left: Nick's Seafood Pavilion, Yorktown, Virginia (painting by Audrey Preissler); lower left: Pine Tree Inn, Virginia Beach, Virginia (painting by Kenneth Harris); lower right: Greenbrier, White Sulphur Springs, West Virginia (painting by Larry Tople)

# North Central

To their tradition of plain cooking rendered superb by the sheer freshness and high quality of local ingredients, the North Central states have added new touches—thanks to modern shipping methods. Thus the traveler in northern Wisconsin may find his trout served either plain or stuffed with lobster and crab. Gilbert Di Cicco's painting of Great Lakes sand dunes is a pleasant setting for some of the staples of this region.

# Army and Lu's

One of the oldest soul food houses in Chicago is Army and Lu's at 422 East 75th Street on the South Side. A cocktail lounge and restaurant, it draws customers from all over the city. Owners William and Luvilla Armstrong have been serving soul for 27 years, "and that is long before anybody called it soul."

Their chef, Allen Pickens, has been on the job about 35 years, beginning as a bus boy while learning the ins and outs of the oven. His specialties include braised oxtails (below) and smoked ham hocks with beans. On rare occasions there are barbecued ribs on the menu.

### BRAISED OXTAILS

3 lb. oxtails
2 cups stewed tomatoes      5 cups beef stock
1 bay leaf      Dash of Worcestershire Sauce
3 cups diced carrots      3 cups diced celery
1 green pepper, diced and seeded
1 large onion, chopped
1 clove garlic, finely minced
1 cup cooked new peas
3 tbsp. cornstarch      Salt and pepper

Disjoint oxtails with a knife to prevent bone fragments from splintering.

Bake them in a 400° oven for 1 hour to render fat. Turn every 15 to 20 minutes until oxtails are browned on all sides. Put in a large pot with tomatoes, beef stock, bay leaf, Worcestershire Sauce, carrots, celery, green pepper, onion, garlic and salt and pepper to taste. Braise until tender, about 2 hours.

When almost done, thicken with cornstarch moistened with a little water. Garnish with new peas. Serves 6 to 8.

# Empire Room, Palmer House

One of 8 restaurants in the Palmer House Hotel at 17 East Monroe Street, Chicago, this elegant dining room has been famous for its food and atmosphere for decades. Open every day for lunch and dinner; reservations necessary.

### BROCHETTE OF CHICKEN ORIENTAL

Bone 6 chicken breasts and remove skin. Remove the tenderloin and cut the remains into 4 tiny tenderloin-shaped strips. Pound each with back of knife. Marinate chicken in mixture of: 1 oz. soy sauce; 2 oz. pineapple juice; ½ tsp. salt; ¼ tsp. Ac'cent (MSG) and ⅛ tsp. black pepper for 1 hour. Let stand 1 hour.

Cut 6 pineapple rings into 5 wedges each. Roll each piece of chicken around a wedge and pin with a metal skewer. Then alternate each chicken roll with 1 piece of water chestnut (1 lb. of water chestnuts will be needed.) Dip each skewer of rolls in melted butter and dredge in 1 cup white bread crumbs. Broil to a golden color and serve on spicy baked rice with Curry Sauce à la Minute. Serves 6.

*Curry Sauce à la Minute:* Combine 2 cups cold water, 1 level tbsp. curry powder, ½ tsp. Ac'cent (MSG), 1 tbsp. chicken base; 1 tbsp. tomato juice; ½ cup apple sauce; ½ tsp. sugar and 1 tbsp. cornstarch moistened with water. Bring mixture to boil.

# Su Casa

In a city famous for fine restaurants, Su Casa is a veritable Mexican jewel box serving the finest Mexican food. It is a replica of a 17th-century hacienda and houses numerous objets d'art and antiques. Located on the near North Side in Chicago, at 49 East Ontario Street, it is open for lunch and dinner daily except Sunday. Reservations advised.

### MOLE DE POLLO

Cook 2 stewing chickens and cut into pieces. Reserve broth. Blend in blender until smooth: ⅓ cup toasted almonds, 10-oz. can tomatillos (green tomatoes), 3 peeled tomatoes, ½ cup toasted pumpkin seeds, 2 oz. Mexican chocolate (or semisweet), and an 8½-oz. jar of Doña Maria Mole en Pasta Sauce. Add a little warm chicken broth.

Combine this mixture with about 2 quarts chicken broth and strain through a coarse sieve. Heat ½ cup of shortening, add strained sauce and simmer until it thickens.

Add salt to taste. Combine with chicken and heat thoroughly. Serves 10. (Check Mexican markets for special ingredients or write to Sol Nadler, c/o La Perferida, 11 Bronx Terminal Market, New York, New York 10451.)

# North Central

Left: Army and Lu's, Chicago, Illinois (photo by Tony Kelly); lower left: Empire Room, Palmer House, Chicago, Illinois (painting by Jim Prindiville); lower right: Su Casa, Chicago, Illinois (painting by Phil Austin)

# The Bakery Restaurant

Louis Szathmary, author of "The Chef's Secret Cook Book," has created a warm and intimate setting here for his excellent 5-course dinners. Open for dinner only, 5 to 11 p.m. Closed Sunday and Monday. Reservations necessary. It is at 2218 North Lincoln Avenue, Chicago.

### ROAST DUCKLING

Rub a 4½-lb. duckling inside and out with chef's salt—a mixture of 1 cup table salt, 1 tbsp. black pepper, 1 tbsp. Hungarian or Spanish paprika and 1 tsp. garlic salt or ¼ tsp. garlic powder. Put 3 generous tbsp. lard, duck fat or chicken fat in a roasting pan.

Place the duckling, breast side down, on the fat. Coarsely dice 1 carrot, 1 medium-sized onion and 2 stalks celery and add 1 or 2 cloves thinly sliced garlic. Sprinkle this mixture inside, on and around the duckling. Add 2 inches of water to the pan, cover tightly and roast in preheated 300° to 325° oven for 2 hours. Cool completely, at room temperature.

Split the duckling lengthwise. Place the 2 halves, skin side up, on a slightly greased cookie sheet in a 425° to 450° oven for 18 to 22 minutes. Before serving remove first 2 joints of wing.

# Tivoli Restaurant

Italian specialties are the attraction here. Tivoli is at 196th Street and Glenwood Road, Chicago Heights, between U.S. 30 and I-294. Open for lunch and dinner every day except Thanksgiving and Christmas. Reservations advisable.

### GNOCCHI

Boil 3 cups water with 1½ tsp. salt and 2 tbsp. butter. Slowly add 1¾ cups French's instant potatoes until water is absorbed. Spread mixture on a large buttered baking sheet to cool. Beat 4 eggs lightly and stir into potatoes. Add 2¾ cups flour; knead until flour is absorbed.

Roll small chunks of dough quickly on well-floured board into finger-thick rolls and cut into 1-inch lengths. Drop a small quantity of gnocchi pieces into 1½ quarts salted boiling water for 10 minutes, stirring. When pieces come to the surface remove them with a slotted spoon. Top with tomato sauce and Parmesan cheese. Serves 8.

# King's Palace Steak House

During the dinner hour there is entertainment and dancing at this restaurant in Lisle, Illinois, a Chicago suburb. It is half a block south of the East-West Tollway and 4 miles west of U.S. 294. Lunch and dinner served daily; reservations necessary.

### LONDON BROIL

Brush a 1-lb. piece of U.S. Choice beef flank with cooking oil, sprinkle with salt and pepper and broil 10 minutes, turn and broil 10 minutes longer for rare, or until done to taste. Carve meat diagonally in thin slices and serve with the burgundy gravy. Serves 4.

*Gravy:* Stir ½ cup burgundy wine into the juices in the dripping pan and brown glaze from broiler; cook. Add 1 tbsp. butter and salt and pepper to taste.

# Willoway Manor

Guests here enjoy leisurely dining in a gracious, century-old home, 1 mile west of Naperville (a Chicago suburb) on Aurora Avenue. Dinner served every day except Mondays and holidays. Reservations not accepted for fewer than 8.

### BLACK BOTTOM PIE

*Crust:* Preheat oven to 325°. Mix 20 crushed gingersnaps with ¼ cup melted butter. Press mixture to bottom and sides of a buttered 10-inch pie pan. Bake 10 minutes at 325°. Cool.

*Filling:* Beat 4 egg yolks with 1½ tbsp. cornstarch dissolved in a little water. Gradually add 2 cups scalded milk and ½ cup sugar. Cook in a double boiler over hot water, stirring frequently, until mixture coats a spoon.

Measure 1½ cups of this mixture and add 2 oz. melted unsweetened chocolate; add 1 tsp. vanilla; blend well. Cool slightly and pour into pie crust. Chill.

Soften 1 tbsp. gelatin in water, add to remaining custard; stir until dissolved. Add 2 tbsp. cognac. Beat 4 egg whites until peaks form, gradually add ½ cup sugar, beat until stiff. Fold into custard. Pour over the chocolate layer, chill. Cover with whipped cream; sprinkle with 3 tbsp. shaved chocolate.

Left: Louis Szathmary of The
Bakery Restaurant, Chicago,
Illinois (photo by Bob Hart);
lower left: King's Palace
Steak House, Lisle, Illinois
(painting by Phil Picard); upper right: Tivoli Restaurant,
Chicago Heights, Illinois
(painting by Sam Hageman);
lower right: Willoway Man-
or, Naperville, Illinois (painting by Mel Kramer)

# Farmer's Daughter

Kandy Henley, a farmer's daughter and former airline stewardess, owns this charming restaurant south of Chicago at 14455 La Grange Road (U.S. 45) in Orland Park, Illinois. Open for dinner every day 5 to 10 p.m.; Sunday noon to 9 p.m. Closed Mondays from Christmas week to Easter. Reservations advisable on weekends.

## OLD-FASHIONED LEMON RAISIN PIE

Soak 2 cups raisins overnight in 2 cups cold water with ½ lemon cut into razor-thin slices. Drain, saving water. Add to it ¼ tsp. salt, ½ cup sugar and 2 tbsp. tapioca. Cook and stir over medium heat until thick. Add raisins and pour into 9-inch unbaked pie shell. Top with lattice strips of crust. Bake at 425° for 35 minutes.

# Vagabond Inn

This is a complete vacation resort in northern Illinois, with 4 dining rooms. All meals served daily. Reservations suggested for meals and lodging. It is on U.S. 51 in Rochelle.

## DATE NUT TORTE

Beat 3 egg yolks well and combine with ½ lb. powdered sugar. Add 1 tsp. baking powder, 2 tbsp. bread crumbs, ½ cup walnuts and 2 cups chopped dates. Fold into 2 stiffly beaten egg whites with 1 tsp. vanilla. Bake in greased shallow pan at 375° for 20 minutes. Serve crumbled or in squares topped with whipped cream. Serves 8.

# Cafe Johnell

John Spillson is the guiding spirit here, serving fine French dishes in elegant Victorian dining rooms. It is at 2529 South Calhoun in Fort Wayne, Indiana. Open weekdays for lunch and dinner; Saturday, dinner only, 5 to 12 p.m. Reservations advisable. Closed Sunday and holidays.

## TROUT SOUFFLÉ

Remove meat from skin of four 6-oz. boned trout, leaving head, tail and skin intact. Put fish meat through grinder or chop very fine. Combine 4 egg whites, 2 tsp. salt, ½ tsp. pepper and ½ tsp. nutmeg with fish and beat mixture at high speed until thickened to a paste. Add 2 cups whipping cream; whip at highest speed until mixture resembles dough. Stuff into trout skins. Refrigerate 30 minutes to 24 hours.

Place fish on buttered pan, brush with butter, sprinkle lightly with paprika and bake at 450° for 15 minutes. Trout will puff up. Remove from oven, garnish with parsley and lemon, and pour sauce over top.

*Sauce:* Clarify 1 cup of sweet butter and brown it slowly, add ¼ cup tomato juice and the juice of 1 lemon. Simmer 5 minutes.

## FROZEN JOHNELLS

Soak 7 or 8 crumbled macaroon cookies in 1 cup of brandy combined with 1 cup of sugar. Whip 1 quart of whipping cream until stiff. Fold whipped cream into the macaroon mixture. Spoon into champagne glasses and freeze for 1 hour. Serves 8.

# La Tour

Atop the 35-story Indiana National Bank Tower, at One Indiana Square, in Indianapolis, La Tour features Continental dishes. Lunch and dinner served daily (no luncheon on Saturday); closed on Sunday. Reservations necessary.

## CREVETTES EN CAISSETTE ROTHSCHILD

*Croustades:* Trim crusts from a loaf of white bread and cut slices 1 inch thick. Leaving an edge of about ¼ inch on all sides, cut pockets into the slices ½ inch deep. Cut out the insides. Sauté croustades in 2 tbsp. peanut oil and ¼ cup unsalted butter until golden brown. Keep hot.

Shell 1 lb. shrimp, set aside. Blend shells in a blender with 1 cup water or fish stock. In a saucepan heat 2 tbsp. peanut oil and ¼ cup unsalted butter, and cook 2 tbsp. chopped shallots, 1 medium onion chopped, and 1 cubed carrot. Add shrimp shell paste. Cook over medium heat for a few minutes. Add 1 tbsp. tomato paste, 1 cup Chablis. Cover, simmer 20 minutes.

Strain sauce into another pan and cook until reduced to about ¾ cup. Stir in 2 tbsp. whipping cream and 1 oz. cognac; bring to boil. Sauté shrimp in another pan in butter for 5 minutes. Place shrimp in croustades and cover with sauce. Brown quickly under broiler. An appetizer for 4.

Upper left: Farmer's Daughter, Orland Park, Illinois (painting by Phil Austin); lower left: John Spillson of Cafe Johnell, Fort Wayne, Indiana (photo by Frank Trebbin); upper right: Vagabond Inn, Rochelle, Illinois (painting by Alex Yaworski); lower right: La Tour, Indianapolis, Indiana (painting by Elroy Grady)

## Johnny and Kay's Hyatt House

This luxury motor hotel with 9 beautiful dining rooms offers midwestern favorites as well as Continental cuisine. Breakfast, lunch and dinner served. It is at 6215 Fleur Drive, Des Moines, Iowa, opposite the airport.

### OLD-FASHIONED POT ROAST

4 lb. beef shoulder or chuck cut
3 onions, diced or sliced    ½ tsp. paprika
2 cloves of garlic, minced    4 bay leaves
1 carrot, sliced    10 peppercorns
1 stalk celery, diced    1 tiny red pepper
1 green pepper, diced    3 tbsp. chicken fat
1½ cups soup stock or tomato juice
2 tbsp. brown sugar    2 tbsp. salt

Braise meat in heavy pot until evenly browned. Add remaining ingredients, cover and simmer 1½ to 2 hours. Strain gravy and thicken to taste. The roast can also be done in a pressure cooker, reducing liquid to half the amount.

## Round-Up Room

A real cowboy atmosphere prevails in this dining room with wagon wheel chandeliers, reindeer heads, ox yoke lanterns and tapestries on the walls depicting Western scenes. Dinner served only, 5 to 11 p.m. Closed Sundays and holidays. It is at 703 13th Avenue, S.E. (State Highway 136), just two blocks north of U.S. 20, in Dyersville, Iowa.

### BEEF STROGANOFF AND NOODLES

2½ lb. beef tenderloin tips, cut julienne style
1 large onion and 1 green pepper, minced
1 oz. brandy    1 tsp. pepper
2 tsp. salt    3 cups beef stock
1½ tsp. garlic salt and celery salt, combined
½ cup dry sherry wine
1 lb. medium noodles, cooked

Brown tips, onions and green pepper in oil. Add other ingredients except noodles and bring to a boil. Thicken with flour and water to desired consistency. Place in 4-inch-deep roasting pan, cover with foil, bake at 325° for 90 minutes. Serve over noodles. Serves 12.

## Hoover House

Red-checkered tablecloths, a massive fireplace and a typical Iowa bill of fare contribute to the provincial atmosphere of this West Branch, Iowa, restaurant. It is in what was once the stone cellar of a century-old Quaker general store. Closed Monday. Tuesday through Saturday: lunch 11 a.m. to 2 p.m., dinner 6 to 10 p.m. Sunday buffet 11:30 a.m. to 8 p.m. Reservations advisable.

### SOUFFLÉ SANDWICHES

Cut crusts from 12 bread slices and butter each on 1 side. Place 6 slices, buttered side down, in a greased flat pan. Put a slice of ham or cheese (or both) on each and cover with another slice, buttered side up.

Beat 4 eggs slightly, add 2 cups milk, 1 tsp. salt and 1 tsp. paprika. Blend well. Pour over sandwiches and refrigerate for several hours, or overnight. Bake at 350° for 45 minutes. Serve hot with asparagus or mushroom sauce (below).

*Sauce:* Melt 2 tbsp. butter and blend with 2 tbsp. flour. Gradually stir in 1½ cups milk. Cook, stirring constantly until smooth and thick. Season with 1 tsp. salt and ¼ tsp. pepper. Add either ½ lb. sliced mushrooms sautéed in 3 tbsp. butter, or a 9-oz. package of frozen asparagus, cooked and drained. Serve hot over sandwiches.

## Shalea Inn

Patrick Elwell and Fred Geering converted a truckers' restaurant into an Old English dining room. It is near Oakland University and Meadowbrook Theater at 3315 Auburn Road, Auburn Heights, Michigan. Take Adams exit from northbound I-75. Lunch and dinner served weekdays; closed Sunday. Reservations accepted for lunch and weekday dinner; but only for 6:30 or 8:30 p.m. on Friday and Saturday.

### SHALEA MAURICE DRESSING

1 cup sharp salad dressing (with vinegar)
1 cup mayonnaise    4 tsp. grated onion
4 tsp. chopped parsley
2 tbsp. sweet pickle, finely chopped
2 hard-boiled egg yolks, chopped

Combine and refrigerate ingredients. Makes dressing for 5 salads.

Top: Round-Up Room, Dyersville, Iowa (painting by Phil Austin); left: Johnny and Kay's Hyatt House, Des Moines, Iowa (painting by Tom Palmerton); lower left: Hoover House, West Branch, Iowa (painting by Tom Palmerton); below: Shalea Inn, Auburn Heights, Michigan (painting by Robert Taylor)

# Weathervane Inn

Occupying a former flour mill, this attractive restaurant is on U.S. 31 in Charlevoix, Michigan. Open the year around; lunch and dinner daily. Overnight accommodations at the adjacent Weathervane Terrace Motel.

## WEATHERVANE BEEF CASSEROLE

Combine 2 lb. cooked chopped beef, 2 oz. red wine, ½ cup tomato sauce, ½ lb. cooked rice, and salt and pepper to taste; place in lightly greased baking dish. Precook 2 whole green peppers in small amount of oil in 375° oven for about 10 minutes. Skin peppers, clean out insides, cut into strips.

Place a layer of pepper strips, 2 oz. green olives (pitted), and wedges of 3 hard-boiled eggs over meat mixture. Add a second layer of meat, then a layer of uncooked green peas (½ lb.). Boil and mash 2 lb. potatoes, mix with ¼ lb. butter and ½ lb. sharp cheese. Place a layer of potatoes over peas, reserving a small amount for decorating with a pastry bag. Bake at 375° for ½ hour. Serves 8.

# Al Green's Celebrity Room

Theater personalities rub elbows with playgoers, business and ad agency tycoons and others who enjoy good food in this handsome dining room in the Fisher Building, Detroit. Open daily for lunch and dinner, 11:30 a.m. to 1:30 a.m. Closed on Sunday. Reservations advisable.

## SYRON'S IRISH STEW

2 lb. lean lamb, 1½-inch cubes
1½ cups flour     3 tsp. salt
1 tsp. pepper     Lamb, veal or beef drippings
4 medium onions, quartered     1 bay leaf
½ tsp. thyme     4 carrots, sliced thick
3 stalks celery, 1-inch diagonal cut
4 potatoes, quartered

Coat lamb with flour, salt and pepper. Using a heavy Dutch oven, sauté the onions in meat drippings until golden; remove from pan. Sauté coated lamb cubes until brown; add sufficient hot water or stock to cover meat, cover tightly and simmer for 1 hour, skimming occasionally. Add bay leaf, thyme, celery and carrots. Cook gently 20 minutes. Then add potatoes and continue cooking until potatoes are done and meat is tender. Adjust seasonings and thicken if desired. Add chopped parsley to your own dumpling recipe; cook dumplings on top of simmering stew. Garnish with chopped parsley. Serves 4 to 6.

# Eastman's Gaslight Room

Bill and Bev Eastman are the hosts at this 1890s restaurant in downtown Detroit at 441 West Grand River, corner of Bagley. Open weekdays for lunch and dinner; Saturdays, dinner only; closed Sundays and holidays.

## FLAMING MUSHROOM CAPS

20 fresh mushroom caps     2 oz. butter
2 oz. sherry     2 oz. brandy

Melt butter in chafing dish. Add fresh mushrooms and sherry. Simmer until caps are soft. Drain excess juice and save. Add brandy and heat. When brandy is well heated, ignite and baste caps, using long-handled ladle. Return saved juice to pan, heat well and serve over broiled steaks or lamp chops. Makes 4 portions.

# Jim's Garage

A few years ago this swinging downtown Detroit restaurant was part of a multilevel parking building. Today it's noted for its excellent food as well as its delightful automotive décor. At 300 West Larned, it is open weekdays 11:30 a.m. to 9 p.m.; closed weekends and holidays.

## SWISS ONION SOUP

½ cup butter     2 lb. onions, thinly sliced
1½ tsp. paprika     ¾ cup flour
½ cup vegetable oil     ¾ tsp. celery salt
Salt and pepper, to taste     6 cups beef stock
8 oz. dark beer     ½ cup Parmesan cheese
12 slices of bread, buttered, sprinkled with the cheese and paprika, then toasted.

Cook onions in butter until soft. Add paprika. Make a roux by browning oil and flour; add roux, celery salt, pepper and salt to beef stock and simmer for at least 2 hours. Add beer; bring to serving temperature. Pour into soup bowls; add a slice of toast to each and sprinkle with additional Parmesan cheese. Serves 12.

Above: Al Green's Celebrity Room, Detroit, Michigan (painting by Bill Kaston); below: Jim's Garage, Detroit, Michigan (photo by Dean Russell); right: Eastman's Gaslight Room, Detroit, Michigan (painting by James Crabb); lower right: Weathervane Inn, Charlevoix, Michigan (painting by Adele Bichan)

# Top of the Flame

Perched atop the Michigan Consolidated Gas Company Building at 1 Woodward Avenue in downtown Detroit, this Stouffer restaurant affords a magnificent view of the city and the Detroit River. Open weekdays 11 a.m. to midnight; Friday and Saturday to 1 a.m. Closed on Sunday.

### LEMON STRAWBERRY ANGEL CREAM CAKE

Soften 1 tbsp. gelatin in ¼ cup cold water. Beat 6 egg yolks and ¾ cup sugar together until creamy, add ¾ cup fresh lemon juice, continue beating. Cook this mixture in top of double boiler until it thickens slightly. Add softened gelatin. Cool.

Beat 6 egg whites until stiff, slowly add ½ cup sugar, still beating. Fold cooled egg yolk mixture into egg whites. Remove crusts from a medium-sized angel food cake, then pull cake apart in 1-inch pieces, and fold cake into egg mixture. Place in a deep round mold; chill at least 1 hour. Unmold on platter, cover with whipped cream, sprinkle with coconut and decorate with strawberries. Serves 10.

# Yamato

At this authentic Japanese restaurant in downtown Detroit's Leland House Hotel, at the corner of Bagley and Cass, kimono-clad waitresses serve Japanese dishes at regular tables or Japanese style. Open every weekday for lunch and dinner. Saturday, dinner only, 6 p.m. to midnight. Reservations advisable on Friday and Saturday nights.

### TEPPAN YAKI (Mixed Grill)

On a lightly oiled hot griddle quickly grill 12 large raw shrimp, 12 stalks asparagus, 6 slices white onion and 2 cups bean sprouts. Then place on plates; keep warm. Grill six 8-oz. strip steaks to taste.

Cut steaks, shrimp and vegetables into bite-sized pieces so all can be eaten with chopsticks. Make a hot sauce by combining chili sauce, Worcestershire Sauce, crushed sesame seeds and ground hot peppers or grated white radish, in proportions to your taste. Mix this sauce with equal parts of lemon juice and soy sauce. Serve with teppan yaki. Serves 6.

# Point West

This year-around resort west of Holland, Michigan, is located on Lake Macatawa, near Lake Michigan. The dining room is open for breakfast, lunch and dinner every day. Reservations advisable. It is on 32nd Street about 6 miles west of U.S. 31.

### POINT WEST SILK CHOCOLATE PIE

½ lb. butter    ½ lb. powdered sugar
2 squares unsweetened chocolate
1 tsp. vanilla    2 eggs
9-inch baked and cooled pie shell
Whipped cream and shaved chocolate
for topping

Cream butter and add sugar slowly. Add chocolate which has been completely melted and cooled. It is very important that the chocolate be cooled, otherwise it will melt the butter. Add vanilla. Add eggs one at a time and beat at high speed for 4 minutes after each addition. Do not overbeat. Spoon into pie shell and refrigerate for 2 hours. Cut with a hot knife and serve topped with whipped cream and shaved chocolate.

# The Vineyards

An imaginative menu, an excellent wine list and an atmosphere reminiscent of a French chateau characterize Fred Graczyk's restaurant at 29230 Franklin Road in Southfield, a suburb just north of Detroit. Dinner only, from 6 to 11 p.m. Reservations necessary; however no reservations are taken for dinner after the 6 p.m. seating on Saturdays. Closed Sunday, Monday and holidays.

### ROAST PORK WITH SWEET-AND-SOUR SAUCE

Place four 1-lb. center-cut rib (not loin) pork roasts in pan, bone side down, and brown at 450° for 30 minutes. Transfer to deep baking dish. Pour Sweet-and-Sour Sauce (below) over pork and roast at 300° for 2½ hours, or until tender. Baste occasionally. Serve with some sauce ladled over meat and garnished with baked apples. Serves 4.

*Sauce:* Combine 2 cups sugar, 1 cup white distilled vinegar, 2 tbsp. chopped green pepper, 1 cup water, 1 tsp. salt; simmer 5 minutes. Thicken sauce with 4 tsp. cornstarch dissolved in 2 tbsp. water. Add 2 tsp. paprika and a bit of finely chopped parsley. Makes 2 cups.

Top: Yamato, Detroit, Michigan (photo by Ray Krisan); left: Top of the Flame, Detroit, Michigan (painting by Robert Taylor); lower left: Point West, Macatawa, Michigan (painting by Lou McMurray); below: The Vineyards, Southfield, Michigan (painting by Robert Boston)

## Iva's Chicken Dinners

A meal here is reminiscent of dinner at grandmother's house in the country. Iva Ousterhout prepares everything in her spotless kitchen and offers a choice of southern or American fried chicken, steaks and seafoods—plus homemade biscuits, relishes, jams and desserts. Lunch and dinner served daily except Tuesday. Reservations suggested in summer. Closed December 20 to February 1. Iva's is on State Highway 76 in Sterling, Michigan, about 30 miles north of Bay City.

### CORN RELISH

| | |
|---|---|
| 2 dozen ears sweet corn | 1½ quarts sugar |
| 4 cups ground onions | ¼ cup salt |
| 6 green peppers, ground | 1½ tsp. tumeric |
| 4 cucumbers, ground | 4 cups vinegar |

4 cups ground peeled tomatoes
1½ tsp. dry mustard
6 red sweet peppers, ground

Remove corn from ears and combine with remaining ingredients in a large kettle. Boil for 1 hour. Turn into sterile jars, fill to overflowing and seal. Makes about 12 quarts.

### PICKLED BEETS FARM STYLE

Trim 6 bunches of small beets of uniform size (6 or 7 beets to a bunch) leaving 2 inches of stem and the entire root. Cook until tender. Drain, saving 2 cups of the water in which beets were cooked. Plunge the beets into cold water and slip off skins. Remove roots and stems. If only large beets are available, slice them.

Make a syrup by cooking 2 cups vinegar, 2 cups sugar and 2 cups beet water and the following spices tied loosely in cheesecloth: ½ tsp. whole cloves, 1½ tsp. allspice, and 1 tsp. whole black peppers. Stir until the sugar is dissolved. Pour over the beets and simmer 15 minutes. Remove the spices. Pack the beets into sterile jars and fill to overflowing with syrup. Seal and store.

### AMERICAN FRIED CHICKEN

Cut 1 stewing hen into 6 pieces. Boil with 1 onion and 1 tbsp. salt until tender. Drain chicken broth for use in gravy and dressing. Roll chicken pieces in Drake's Batter Mix and fry in hot Crisco until brown. Serves 6.

## The Highland Supper Club

As the name suggests, this intimate dining spot recreates a bit of Scotland with its decorations of Scottish carvings, armor and guns. The tartan-clad waitresses serve from 11 a.m. to 1 a.m. every weekday. Closed on Sunday. Reservations necessary for weekends. Dinner music and dancing every night. The club is just 5 minutes from downtown Duluth, Minnesota, at 1301 Miller Trunk Highway at the junction of U.S. 53 and State Highway 194.

### LOBSTER O'BRIEN

1 lb. fresh uncooked lobster meat
1 small green pepper, chopped
½ cup mushrooms, chopped

| | |
|---|---|
| 1 tbsp. pimento, chopped | 3 oz. butter |
| 1 oz. sherry | Paprika |
| 1 cup white rice, cooked | Parsley |

Cut lobster meat into bite-sized pieces. Combine with chopped pepper, mushrooms and pimento; sauté in melted butter. Add sherry and cook over medium heat about 5 minutes; add paprika for a little color. Make a bed of the hot cooked rice in a casserole. Place cooked lobster mixture on top of rice and garnish with parsley. Serves 2.

## The Blue Horse

In the 10 years it has been in operation, this restaurant, operated by Clifford Warling, has established itself as one of the Twin Cities' outstanding dining places. Open every weekday from 11 a.m. to 1 a.m. Closed on Sunday. Reservations recommended for weekend nights. Located at 1355 University Avenue in St. Paul, Minnesota.

### STRAWBERRY BAVARIAN CREAM

| | |
|---|---|
| 4 eggs, separated | 5 tbsp. sugar |
| 4 tsp. plain gelatin | 1½ cups hot milk |
| ½ cup heavy cream, whipped | Rum |

1 cup strawberries and juice

Beat egg yolks with sugar until light and fluffy. Soak gelatin in ¼ cup cold water 5 minutes and add to yolk mixture. Add hot milk gradually and stir over low heat until gelatin dissolves and mixture thickens enough to coat a metal spoon. Remove from heat and stir until cool. Fold in stiffly beaten egg whites and whipped cream. Add crushed strawberries and berry juice. Sprinkle with rum and chill. Yield: 5 to 6 servings.

Above: Iva's Chicken Dinners, Sterling, Michigan (painting by Max Altekruse); upper right: The Highland Supper Club, Duluth, Minnesota (illustration by Ed Paulson); right: The Blue Horse, St. Paul, Minnesota (painting by Francis Meisch)

# Tony & Luigi's

Tony Alesio owns this supper club which serves Italian-American dishes and also offers nightly entertainment. Dinner is served daily 5 p.m. to 1 a.m., reservations advisable. Closed on Sundays. It is at 5140 "O" Street (U.S. 6) in Lincoln, Nebraska.

## CHICKEN LIVERS À LA MARSALA

1½ lb. chicken livers    2 tbsp. lemon juice
½ cup flour    ¼ cup olive oil
½ cup Marsala wine (or sweet sherry)
2 cups hot rice    Lemon slices

Squeeze a little lemon juice over livers. Roll in flour and sauté gently in olive oil, stirring frequently. After a few minutes add wine and cover pan, simmer over low flame about 5 minutes. Sprinkle with salt and pepper and serve over hot rice, garnished with lemon slices. Serves 4.

# Radisson Blackstone Hotel

The décor in the Orleans Room here is French Provincial, but the food is American at its very best: tender seafood, prime Nebraska beef, meticulously seasoned salads. Open every day for lunch and dinner from 11 a.m. to midnight. The Blackstone is 8 blocks west of I-80 (use Farnam Street Exit) and a block south of U.S. 6, just 5 minutes from downtown Omaha, Nebraska.

## BEEF À LA FRENCH MARKET

2½ lb. sliced beef tenderloin tips
2 tbsp. cooking oil    4 tbsp. flour
½ cup dry red burgundy
2 cups tiny whole carrots    ½ cup shallots
2 cups fresh or frozen peas
1 cup sliced mushrooms
Salt and pepper to taste
6 cups cooked egg noodles

Sauté beef slices in oil until done rare. Take out meat, stir drippings and blend in 4 tbsp. flour. When smooth slowly add enough water (about 2 cups) to make a heavy sauce. Add wine, then precooked vegetables and seasoning and let simmer for 5 minutes. Put beef back in pan and simmer for a couple of minutes. Pour over cooked noodles, garnish with parsley and serve hot. Serves 6.

# Marina Inn

Located at the juncture of 3 states—Iowa, Nebraska and South Dakota - this 8-acre hotel complex on the Missouri River has a marina that accommodates 150 boats. The Swashbuckler (one of its 2 dining rooms) is a luxurious supper club. All meals served daily. The Inn is at 4th and B Streets, South Sioux City, Nebraska. It is 1 block east of U.S. 77, and is easily accessible from U.S. 20, U.S. 75 and I-29.

## RUSSIAN DRESSING

½ cup sugar    2 tsp. salt
¼ cup vinegar    ⅛ tsp. ground cloves
⅓ cup ketchup    1 small minced onion
1 cup salad oil    1 tsp. Worcestershire Sauce
1 clove garlic, cut in quarters

Combine above ingredients and age in refrigerator for a few hours. Take out garlic pieces before serving. Makes 1 pint dressing. At the Inn, Executive Chef Mike Costello serves this dressing on a tossed Boston lettuce salad, garnished with tomato wedges. Shredded red cabbage and carrots are added to salad for color.

# Dreisbach's

For 45 years this steak house in Grand Island, Nebraska, has been popular with both residents and visitors. Family-style dinners—all you can eat—are served to groups of 4 or more. Open for dinner only, 5 p.m. to 1 a.m. The address is 1137 South Locust Street, 6 miles from the Grand Island Exit of I-80.

## DREISBACH'S CHICKEN CACCIATORE

1 chicken, cut up and boned
1 package spaghetti sauce mix    ½ cup flour
1 tbsp. oil    1 tsp. oregano
1 tsp. thyme    1 tsp. sweet basil leaves
1 medium onion, sliced
14½-oz. can stewed tomatoes    ½ cup sauterne

Roll chicken pieces in a mixture of the spaghetti sauce mix and flour. Brown in oil and place in casserole. Combine oregano, thyme, basil, onion and tomatoes; simmer for 5 minutes before pouring over chicken. Bake covered at 350° for 30 minutes. Add sauterne and bake for 20 minutes or more. Serves 4.

Top: Dreisbach's, Grand Island, Nebraska (painting by Tom Palmerton); above: Tony & Luigi's, Lincoln, Nebraska (painting by Tom Palmerton); upper right: Radisson Blackstone Hotel, Omaha, Nebraska (painting by Tom Palmerton); right: Marina Inn, South Sioux City, Nebraska (painting by Mary Rupp)

# The Seven Seas

In the heart of the prairies, in Mandan, North Dakota, this restaurant is dedicated to the "Great Age of Sail" in décor and cuisine. Open every day for breakfast, lunch and dinner which is served until 1 a.m. Reservations advisable for dinner. From I-94 take Exit 31.

## SHRIMP CREOLE

1½ lb. cooked shrimp, whole or cut in pieces
1 onion, chopped fine      ½ cup diced celery
1 green pepper, chopped fine      1 bay leaf
1 tbsp. butter      1 tbsp. flour
3 cups canned tomatoes, chopped      1 tsp. salt
1 tsp. sugar      Pinch of cayenne pepper
½ tsp. garlic powder      ¼ tsp. lemon pepper

Sauté onion, green pepper, celery and bay leaf in butter for 10 minutes or until cooked. Add flour and blend. Add tomatoes, salt, sugar, garlic powder, cayenne and lemon pepper and simmer gently for about 15 minutes. Add shrimp, and continue to simmer until shrimp is thoroughly heated. Serve on hot rice and garnish with ripe olives and lemon wedges. Serves 4 to 6.

# Maisonette

The Maisonette is famous for its exceptional Continental cuisine. It is in downtown Cincinnati at 114 East 6th Street. Open for dinner Monday through Saturday; for lunch, Monday through Friday. Closed most holidays and the first 2 weeks in July. Reservations necessary.

## CRÊPES AUX FRAISES FLAMBÉE

Sift together ⅔ cup flour, 1 tbsp. sugar and a pinch of salt. Beat 2 whole eggs and 2 egg yolks; add to flour mixture. Add 1¾ cups milk, blend smooth. Add 2 tbsp. melted butter and 1 tbsp. rum or cognac. Let batter stand for 2 hours, then make 12 crepes in the usual way.

Mash about 36 strawberries and add 2 tbsp. Cointreau. Melt 6 pats of butter in a large skillet over low heat, cover bottom with Melba Sauce (above), adding a few drops of Cointreau. In the pan, roll each crêpe around 1 tbsp. strawberries. When all are rolled, add Cointreau to pan and ignite. Place 2 crêpes on each plate; spoon sauce over them; place 1 tbsp. ice cream on 1 side of crêpe and 1 tbsp. whipped cream on the other, topped with a whole berry. Serves 6.

*Melba Sauce:* Blend: 4 tbsp. strawberry preserves; 2 tbsp. currant jelly; 2 tbsp. red food coloring; 1 tbsp. strawberry extract.

# The Hollenden Tavern

An elegant and cosmopolitan dining room, the Hollenden Tavern is at 610 Superior Street, N.E., in Cleveland. All meals served daily. Reservations necessary except for breakfast.

## SAUERKRAUT BALLS

4 oz. cooked pork      4 oz. corned beef
4 oz. ham      1 small onion, chopped fine
Pinch of chopped parsley      1 cup flour
½ tsp. dry mustard      ½ tsp salt
1 cup milk      1 lb. sauerkraut
2 eggs, beaten      1 cup bread crumbs
Deep fat for frying

Run meats through a grinder on medium or fine; add onion and parsley. Fry this mixture until brown. Combine flour, mustard and salt; sift once. Add to meat, then add milk. Cook until fluffy. Cool, then add to sauerkraut.

Put entire meat mixture through a grinder twice, mixing thoroughly. Roll into 1½-inch balls, dredge in flour, dip in egg, roll in bread crumbs and fry in deep fat. Serve hot as an appetizer.

# Fountas' 16 East

This popular restaurant in Columbus, Ohio, is noted for excellent food. Open for lunch and dinner every day except Sunday; dinner only on Saturday. The address is 16 East Broad Street.

## STEAK DIANE

Broil four 4-oz. slices of beef tenderloin, flattened, on both sides until rare. Combine ¾ cup chopped green onions (with tops), ¾ cup sliced canned or fresh mushrooms and ½ tsp. minced fresh garlic and heat well in a saucepan in 3 pats of butter (do not brown).

Add the steaks and cook 1 minute on each side. Add ½ tsp. Worcestershire Sauce and then ½ tsp. brandy. This will cause steaks to flame. Remove from heat and pour on ½ cup rich beef broth. Remove steaks to serving platters; cook sauce for about 1 minute more and spoon over steaks. Serves 2.

Top: The Seven Seas, Mandan, North Dakota (painting by Gary P. Miller); left: Maisonette, Cincinnati, Ohio (painting by Charles Harper); lower left: The Hollenden Tavern, Cleveland, Ohio (painting by John Baird); below: Fountas' 16 East, Columbus, Ohio (painting by Ned Moore)

# Cranston's

Owners Charles Hess and Bruce Pachete serve gourmet food in a homey, friendly atmosphere at 15245 Lincoln Street S. E. (U.S. 30), ½ mile west of Minerva, Ohio. Open weekdays 5 to 8:30 p.m.; Saturday 5 to 9 p.m.; Sunday 11 a.m. to 8 p.m. Closed Monday and the last week of July.

### DATE NUT PUDDING

|  |  |
|---|---|
| 1 tbsp. flour | 1 tsp. baking powder |
| 1 cup dates, chopped | 1 cup pecans, chopped |
| 2 eggs | ⅔ cup sugar |
| 1 tsp. vanilla | Pinch of salt |
| 1 cup whipping cream, whipped | |

Sift flour and baking powder and mix well with dates and nuts. Beat eggs, then add sugar, vanilla and salt. Put date mixture in greased 10-inch pie pan, pour egg mixture over and mix well in pan. Bake at 350° for 30 minutes. Cool and serve topped with whipped cream. Serves 7.

# Powder House Lodge

This lodge is only 3 miles from Mt. Rushmore National Memorial, with mountain lakes, trout streams, and ghost towns also nearby. Overnight accommodations. Open May 15 to September 15; reservations advisable. The dining room is open daily 6 to 11 a.m. and 5 to 9 p.m. (no lunch). It is on U.S. 16 in Keystone, South Dakota.

### MARINATED BEEF STRIPS

|  |  |
|---|---|
| Leftover cooked, cold roast beef | |
| 2 cups water | 1½ tsp. salt |
| 6 oz. red wine vinegar | 1½ bay leaves |
| 1 onion, sliced thin | ¼ cup brown sugar |
| ¼ tsp. crushed peppercorns | |
| 1 clove garlic, chopped | 3 whole cloves |

Cut beef in pieces ⅛-inch thick and ⅜-inch wide. The stripping must be done across the grain of the meat. Combine other ingredients, add to beef strips and marinate in refrigerator for at least 48 hours. Drain and serve as a cold appetizer.

# Kirk's Restaurant

For over 30 years the Kirk brothers—George, Larry, Ted and Chris—have operated this hospitable, family-type restaurant at 2605 West 12th Street, 1 mile east of I-29 in Sioux Falls, South Dakota. Open daily from 5 a.m. to 2 a.m. for breakfast, lunch, dinner and late evening supper.

### BAKED CHICKEN OREGANATI

|  |  |
|---|---|
| 4 chickens halved (2 to 2½ lb.) | 1 tsp. oregano |
| ⅓ lb. melted butter | Salt and pepper, to taste |
| Juice of 2 lemons or ⅓ cup lemon juice concentrate | |

Lay chicken halves on roasting pan and brush with melted butter. Bake at 400° for about 15 minutes or until brown. Blend the rest of the melted butter with lemon juice and oregano and heat slightly. Add salt and pepper to taste. Pour 1 cup water in the bottom of the baking pan to give proper steaming. Reduce heat to 300° and bake chicken for about 1 hour, basting with butter mixture at 20-minute intervals. Serves 8.

# Wilson's Town 'n Country

Good German and American dishes are served in this restaurant at 2104 West 12th street (U.S. 16) in Sioux Falls, South Dakota. Open daily, 7 a.m. to 10 p.m. Closed Christmas Day.

### LIVER DUMPLINGS (Lederknödel)

|  |  |
|---|---|
| 5 slices white bread | 1 cup lukewarm milk |
| ¾ lb. beef liver, or ½ lb. beef liver and ¼ lb. pork liver | |
| 2 oz. kidney fat | 1 small onion |
| 2 eggs | Generous pinch of marjoram |
| 1 tsp. salt | Grated rind of 1 lemon |
| Breadcrumbs | 1½ quarts beef broth |

Break or cut bread into small pieces. Cover with warm milk and soak until milk becomes cool. Squeeze to remove excess milk. Using fine blade, grind bread, liver, kidney fat and onion together. Mix in eggs, salt, marjoram and lemon rind. Add bread crumbs, a tablespoonful at a time, until mixture can be handled sufficiently to shape into 18 2-inch dumplings. Shape with wet hands. Simmer dumplings in broth 20 minutes; serve in broth.

POWDER HOUSE
MOTEL FINE FOOD

Top: Cranston's, Minerva, Ohio (painting by Robert Taylor); above: Kirk's Restaurant, Sioux Falls, South Dakota (painting by Frank Saso); upper right: Powder House Lodge, Keystone, South Dakota (painting by Lou McMurray); lower right: Wilson's Town 'n Country, Sioux Falls, South Dakota (painting by Harvey Kidder)

**OHIO/SOUTH DAKOTA 79**

# "Babe" Van Camp's Club

For over 30 years "Babe's" in northern Wisconsin's resort country has been popular for its excellent food and friendly atmosphere. It is on South Memorial Drive (State Highway 47) in Appleton, 1 block south of U.S. 10. Open weekdays for lunch and dinner; Saturdays and Sundays from 5 p.m.

### LETTUCE AND SPINACH WITH SWEET-SOUR BACON DRESSING

| | |
|---|---|
| 6 to 8 slices bacon | ½ tsp. salt |
| 1 head lettuce | Dash pepper |
| Crisp spinach, to blend | ½ cup cider vinegar |
| 3 tsp. sugar | ½ cup sliced scallions (optional) |

Cut bacon into small pieces, sauté until crisp, drain on paper towel, saving fat. In a large salad bowl break lettuce into bite-size pieces. Add enough spinach to blend, and scallions if desired. Add bacon bits. Toss.

Add sugar, salt, pepper and vinegar to 2 tbsp. of the bacon fat and bring to a boil. Pour over greens and toss until each leaf is coated. Serve at once. Serves 6 to 8.

# Telemark Lodge

In the heart of the lake and forest region of northwestern Wisconsin, Telemark provides a diversity of recreation and complete vacation facilities. All meals served daily; reservations advisable. It is 3 miles east of Cable, off Highway M.

### BROOK TROUT VERONIQUE

4 brook trout (8 oz.), cleaned, with head left on
½ cup small lobster chunks     1 oz. white wine
½ cup crabmeat
½ cup sautéed sliced mushrooms
1 chicken bouillon cube, in 1 cup hot water
4 oz. American cheese, grated

Mix all ingredients except trout to make a stuffing; put into trout cavities. Flour trout and dip in beaten egg. Brown in butter with a small amount of Worcestershire Sauce. Bake at 400° about 20 minutes until done.

*Garnish:* Melt 1 tbsp. butter and add 2 dashes Worcestershire Sauce. Dribble this over top of trout. Add a few canned white seedless grapes (or poached fresh grapes) that have been sautéed lightly in butter.

# Jimmie's Del-Bar

For many years the Wimmer family has owned and operated this restaurant in Lake Delton, Wisconsin. On U.S. 12, it is 2 miles north of I-90. Lunch served daily from Memorial Day through Labor Day; dinner served all year from 4:30 to midnight. Reservations advisable.

### BREAST OF CAPON AU SHERRY

Sauté 2 boned breasts of capon in butter until lightly brown. Add 1 cup chicken stock, cover and simmer 15 minutes or until tender. Served on rice pilaf topped with sauce (below). Serves 2.

*Sherry Mushroom Sauce:* Slice 4 oz. of fresh mushrooms and sauté in clarified butter. Brown 3 tbsp. flour in 2 tbsp. butter, add ½ cup meat stock, and cook until thickened, stirring constantly. Sauté 1 tbsp. chopped onion and 3 tbsp. chopped green pepper in 2 tbsp. butter and add to sauce. Add 3 chopped ripe olives, mushrooms, salt and pepper to taste, and 2 tbsp. dry sherry.

# Golden Zither

Melodies played on the zither add to guests' pleasure in this charming German restaurant from which live radio broadcasts featuring singing waitresses have emanated for years. Open daily for lunch, dinner and supper. Reservations advisable. Closed on Christmas Eve. It is at 50th and Vliet streets in downtown Milwaukee.

### HASENPFEFFER

Cut 1 large dressed rabbit in serving pieces. Let stand at least 24 hours, refrigerated, in a marinade of:

| | |
|---|---|
| 2 cups white vinegar | 1 tbsp. salt |
| 1 cup water | 1 tsp. pepper, freshly ground |
| 1 cup claret | 10 cloves |
| 2 large onions, sliced | 6 bay leaves |
| 2 tbsp. brown sugar | |

Remove rabbit pieces from marinade and brown in a large skillet. Bring marinade to a boil. Lightly brown 2 tbsp. flour in 3 tbsp. fat in a small skillet, thicken marinade. Strain gravy and pour over rabbit. Simmer until tender.

Top: "Babe" Van Camp's Club, Appleton, Wisconsin (painting by Robert Taylor); center: Telemark Lodge, Cable, Wisconsin (painting by Gary P. Miller); left: Jimmie's Del-Bar, Lake Delton, Wisconsin (painting by Al Anderson); above: Golden Zither, Milwaukee, Wisconsin (painting by Bruce Bond)

# South Central

Though grouped together as the South Central states, these regions vary widely in terrain, temperament and traditions—a diversity that is reflected in their foods. The fortunate traveler has a broad choice of dishes, from the perhaps-expected Western chili to the super-steaks of Kansas and the elegant French cooking of New Orleans. Behind this arrangement of Southern delicacies is a painting by Clarence Kincaid.

83

# Red Apple Inn

Perched atop a mountain and surrounded by acres of woods and lakes, this resort offers golf, fishing, sailing, swimming and tennis. Breakfast, lunch and dinner served daily. It is in Eden Isle on State Highway 110, 4 miles west of Heber Springs, in central Arkansas. Reservations advisable.

## CHICKEN BREASTS, EDEN ISLE

6 chicken breasts, halved      Pepper
12 bacon slices      Package of dried beef
2 cans cream of chicken soup
1½ cups sour cream      3 oz. cream cheese
4 cups hot rice

Pepper, but do *not* salt, chicken breasts. Wrap 1 slice of bacon around each half. Place a layer of dried beef (not corned beef) in the bottom of baking dish. Arrange bacon-wrapped chicken on beef slices. Combine chicken soup, sour cream and cream cheese; pour over chicken. Cover pan tightly with foil.

Place in 325° oven for two hours. When meat is tender remove foil and let brown slightly. Serve on bed of hot rice. Serves 12.

## EGGPLANT MUSHROOM CASSEROLE

Peel and slice 3 eggplants; soak in salted water 1 hour; pour off water. Boil until tender; drain; set aside in mixing bowl.

Sauté 1 cup finely minced onions slowly in 1½ tbsp. olive oil or butter for about 10 minutes until tender but not browned. Season lightly with salt and pepper and add to eggplant.

Twist 1 lb. finely minced fresh mushrooms, a handful at a time, in a towel to extract juice. (Or use canned mushrooms.) Sauté them in 3 tbsp. butter and 1 tbsp. olive oil until very lightly browned (5 to 6 minutes). Season with salt and pepper; add to eggplant.

Mash 4½ oz. cream cheese, then beat it into eggplant mixture. Beat in 4 tbsp. minced parsley and ½ tsp. basil or ¼ tsp. thyme. Put eggplant mixture in casserole, top with 3 tbsp. grated Swiss cheese mixed with 3 tbsp. fine dry bread crumbs; baste with 2 to 3 tbsp. melted butter.

Place casserole in pan with ⅛ inch water; bake at 375° for 25 to 30 minutes to heat thoroughly and to brown topping. Serves 8.

# Crossbow

Located on State Highways 68 and 23, this restaurant owned by Betty and Wilma Ledbetter is about a quarter-mile northeast of Huntsville in northwestern Arkansas. Breakfast, buffet lunch and dinner served; hours 6 a.m. to 8:30 p.m. Closed on Monday. Reservations advisable during the football season and weekends.

## GERMAN'S CHOCOLATE CAKE

Melt 1 package (4 oz.) German's Sweet Chocolate in ½ cup boiling water. Cool. Cream 1 cup butter and 2 cups sugar until fluffy. Add 4 unbeaten egg yolks, one at a time, and beat well after each. Add melted chocolate and 1 tsp. vanilla. Mix well.

Sift together ½ tsp. salt, 1 tsp. baking soda, 2½ cups cake flour. Add alternately with 1 cup buttermilk to chocolate mixture, beating well. Beat until smooth. Fold in 4 stiffly beaten egg whites. Pour into three 8- or 9-inch cake layer pans, lined on bottom with waxed paper. Bake in moderate oven (350°) for 30 to 40 minutes. Cool. Fill layers and frost top with coconut-pecan frosting (below).

*Coconut-Pecan Frosting:* Combine 1 cup evaporated milk, 1 cup sugar, 3 egg yolks and 1 stick butter. Add 1 tsp. vanilla. Cook over low heat, stirring constantly, until thickened (about 14 minutes). Add 1⅓ cups coconut and 1 cup chopped pecans. Beat until thick enough to spread.

Above: Red Apple Inn, Eden Isle, Arkansas (painting by Max Altekruse); right: Crossbow, Huntsville, Arkansas (painting by Ron Miles)

# Town and Country

The central location of this family resort and restaurant in the Beaver Lake area makes it an ideal headquarters for vacationists who want to take scenic tours or fishing trips and enjoy the other recreation facilities of northwestern Arkansas. It is on U.S. 71 and 62, south of Rogers. The dining room features a daily buffet with a choice of several meat courses, 21 salads and a selection of homemade baked goods. Breakfast, lunch and dinner served daily; overnight accommodations. Reservations advised for rooms during the summer.

## BACON BEAN SALAD

<pre>
⅔ cup cider vinegar        ¾ cup sugar
  1 tsp. salt     1-lb. can cut green beans
1-lb. can cut wax beans      1-lb. can lima beans
  1-lb. can kidney beans, rinsed and drained
   1 medium-sized onion, quartered and
                 sliced fine
  1 medium-sized green pepper, chopped
      ½ tsp. freshly ground pepper
      ⅓ cup salad oil      Lettuce
 1 lb. unsliced bacon, cut in 1-inch cubes
</pre>

Blend vinegar, sugar and salt in a small saucepan. Heat until the sugar is dissolved and set aside. Drain all beans and toss with onion, green pepper, vinegar mixture and pepper. Pour oil over all and toss to coat evenly. Store in a large covered container in refrigerator for at least 8 hours. When ready to serve, fry bacon until crisp, and dry it on absorbent paper. Toss the bacon with the bean mixture. Place portions in lettuce cups. Serves 12.

# Brookville Hotel

The sign over the door to the kitchen reads, "Only Good Food and Pleasant People Pass Through This Door." Built in 1870, this establishment boasts the same family operation since 1897. An excellent family-style dinner has been served here for the past 57 years, complete with all the old-fashioned trimmings. It is on State Highway 140 in Brookville, Kansas, 7 miles south of I-70. Dinner served every day except Monday. Reservations necessary. Closed Thanksgiving and Christmas Day.

## CARAMELS

In a heavy pan combine: one 15-oz. can Eagle Brand condensed milk (this is *not* evaporated milk), ½ cup coffee cream, 1 cup light Karo syrup, 2 cups sugar, 1 cup sweet milk and ¼ cup butter. Cook, stirring constantly, to 245° on candy thermometer, or to firm ball stage in cold water.

Remove from fire, add 2 tsp. vanilla. Pour half of mixture into buttered 8-inch pan, then sprinkle surface with 1 cup broken pecans. Add remaining caramel mixture.

When firm, invert candy onto a board and cut it with a thin knife. Refrigerate for 2 hours. Wrap pieces in waxed paper.

# The Village Restaurant

Fine Italian cuisine and warm hospitality are the hallmarks of this 26-year-old restaurant operated by the Vincent Distefano family. Located at 8464 Airline Highway on the east side of Baton Rouge, Louisiana, it is open for lunch and dinner every day except Monday. Closed on some holidays.

## BRUCCIALUNA

<pre>
 2 veal round steaks, cut ¼-inch thick
       3 tbsp. Italian cheese, grated
 ⅛ tsp. basil leaf     1 clove garlic, minced
    ⅛ tsp. oregano (more may be added)
1 small onion, minced      2 cups bread crumbs
 Salt and pepper, to taste      ¼ cup olive oil
            2 cups tomato sauce
</pre>

Cut prepared steaks in half. Mix dry ingredients and moisten with olive oil. Spread dressing on steaks, roll and secure with strong picks or skewers. Braise in skillet for 15 minutes. Turn steak rolls to keep from burning. Drop steaks into your favorite tomato sauce. Cook about 30 minutes. Serves 4.

Top: Town and Country, Rogers, Arkansas (illustration by Will Slocum); left: Brookville Hotel, Brookville, Kansas (painting by Tom Palmerton); below: The Village Restaurant, Baton Rouge, Louisiana (painting by Jim Musser)

# Masson's Restaurant Français

About five miles west of I-10 and U.S. 61, this fine French restaurant is at 7200 Pontchartrain Boulevard, about 7 miles northwest of downtown New Orleans.

## QUICHE LORRAINE

9-inch pie shell, 2 inches deep
3 eggs      1½ cups heavy cream
1 tbsp. flour      Salt and pepper to taste
3 oz. Swiss cheese, sliced thin
½ lb. bacon, chopped and partially cooked

Bake the pie shell partially (4 to 6 minutes at 350°). Beat eggs and combine with cream. Add flour, salt and pepper. Arrange slices of cheese on bottom of pie shell. Cover with bacon. Pour egg and cream mixture over slowly. Bake at 350° for 30 to 40 minutes, or until silver knife inserted comes out clean. About 8 servings.

## SABAYON

6 eggs separated      ¾ cup heavy cream
¾ cup sugar      1 tsp. vanilla
¾ cup cream sherry

Beat yolks with sugar until creamy. Add sherry and cook in double boiler until thick. Cool in bowl 10 to 15 minutes. Add stiffly whipped cream and vanilla. Fold in stiffly beaten egg whites. Divide into 8 ramekins and chill 3 to 4 hours. Serves 8.

# Pontchartrain Hotel

In a city noted for excellent food, the Caribbean Room in the Hotel Pontchartrain is considered one of the finest eating places. Lunch served noon to 2 p.m., dinner from 6 to 10 p.m. every day. Reservations suggested. The address is 2031 St. Charles Avenue in uptown New Orleans.

## OYSTERS ODETTE ON HALF SHELL

3 doz. oysters      5 shallots, chopped fine
2 tbsp. butter      2 tbsp. flour
1 tbsp. Worcestershire Sauce      ½ tsp. salt
½ tsp. prepared mustard      Few grains cayenne
⅛ tsp. nutmeg      ½ tsp. chopped parsley
2½-oz. can mushrooms, chopped
1 egg yolk      Buttered cracker crumbs

Wash and chop oysters. Cook shallots in butter; add flour and brown. Add the rest of the seasonings and parsley, oysters and mushrooms. Cook 5 minutes over medium fire. Remove and add egg yolk. Put mixture in deep halves of oyster shells, cover with crumbs and bake in 350° oven for 15 minutes. Serves 6 as an appetizer.

# Smith's Cross Lake Inn

Authentic seashells, seahorses, hanging fishnets, and an 8-foot sailfish adorn the walls of this restaurant which overlooks Louisiana's beautiful Cross Lake. The owners, Mr. and Mrs. Glenn Smith, claim their seafood fare is excellent—and patrons agree. Located at 5301 South Lakeshore Drive in Shreveport, Louisiana, it is open for dinner daily except Sunday. Reservations are preferred.

## GREEN BEANS FRENCH STYLE

1 cup ground, toasted bread crumbs
4 cups cooked, French-style green beans
1 cup sour cream
½ cup grated Parmesan cheese
Salt and pepper, to taste

Sprinkle a thin layer of bread crumbs in a greased casserole. Then add 1 layer each of beans, sour cream and cheese. Season with salt and pepper. Repeat these steps until all ingredients are used. Bake at 400° for 15 minutes or until heated through. Serves 4.

## STRAWBERRY DELIGHT

Sprinkle 1 cup powdered sugar over 1 quart whole fresh strawberries which have been washed and hulled. Toss gently. Chill in refrigerator for 1 hour, stirring occasionally.

Whip 1 cup whipping cream, add 1 tsp. almond extract and 2 tsp. orange juice. Fold whipped cream mixture into berries and serve at once. Serves 4.

Top: Masson's Restaurant Français, New Orleans, Louisiana (painting by Don Smith); center: Pontchartrain Hotel, New Orleans, Louisiana (painting by Adele Bichan); right: Smith's Cross Lake Inn, Shreveport, Louisiana (painting by James Crabb)

# Tiak O'Khata Restaurant

The bountiful cuisine that made Southern home cooking justifiably famous is one of the irresistible attractions of this resort complex owned and managed by Mrs. Sylvester Smyth and Mrs. Sylvia White. It is in Louisville, Mississippi, 30 miles from the Natchez Trace Parkway and 1 mile from State Highway 15 on Smyth Road. Open the year around, it offers overnight accommodations as well as boating, fishing and swimming for vacationers. The dining room is open for breakfast, lunch and dinner from 8 a.m. to 9:30 p.m. Reservations advisable.

### PEAR PRESERVE CAKE

| | |
|---|---|
| 2 cups sugar | 1 cup butter |
| 2½ cups flour | 4 eggs |
| 1 tsp. soda | 1 tsp. salt |
| 1 tsp. nutmeg | 1 tsp. cinnamon |
| 1 tsp. cloves | 1 cup buttermilk |
| 1 tsp. vanilla | 1 cup pecans, chopped |
| 1 cup raisins | 1 cup pear (or peach) preserves |

Cream butter and sugar thoroughly. Beat in eggs, one at a time. Reserve ½ cup of flour. Sift remaining dry ingredients together.

Alternately add dry ingredients and buttermilk. Add vanilla. Dredge nuts and raisins in remaining ½ cup of flour, add to batter. Stir in preserves. Pour into 3 paper-lined, deep 9-inch layer pans (or a large sheet cake pan). Bake for about 25 minutes at 350°.

*Topping:* Combine 2 cups sugar, ½ cup cream, 4 tbsp. white Karo syrup and ¼ lb. butter. Cook to soft ball stage and pour over cake while both cake and topping are hot to saturate layers or sheet cake.

### TURKEY DRESSING CASSEROLE

Crumble 2 cups cornbread and 2 yeast rolls in a bowl. Soften with 2 cups warm, seasoned, rich turkey broth.

Blend ½ cup buttermilk, 2 medium-sized onions (quartered) and ¼ tsp. soda in blender. Add to crumb mixture, stir in 4 well-beaten eggs, ½ cup melted turkey fat (or butter) and 1 tbsp. celery seed. Pour into well-greased 9 x 12-inch pan and bake at 350° until brown, about 1 hour. Serve hot with giblet gravy.

# Mendenhall Hotel

Three huge round dining tables, each with a revolving lazy Susan center portion covered with a wonderful variety of food, are a unique feature of this 60-year-old family-operated hotel. Lunch served from 11 a.m. to 2 p.m. and dinner 6 to 7:30 p.m. Dining room closed Sunday evening only. Overnight accommodations. It is on U.S. 49, in the center of Mendenhall, Mississippi, which is 30 miles southeast of Jackson.

### RICE CASSEROLE

Melt ¼ lb. butter in a pan. Sauté 4 chopped green onions in butter until they are light brown. Add 2 cans mushroom soup and juice from a 4-oz. can of mushrooms. Blend together. Pour this mixture over 4 cups of cooked rice in a casserole. Then add a layer of 10 oz. of grated sharp cheese, drained 4-oz. can of mushrooms, and 1 cup of chopped toasted almonds. Bake in 350° oven until casserole is heated through. Serves 10.

### HARVARD BEETS

| | |
|---|---|
| 1 No. 2 can sliced beets | ½ cup white sugar |
| ½ cup white vinegar | 1 level tbsp. cornstarch |

Dissolve cornstarch in beet juice. Add to remaining ingredients and cook over slow heat until glazed, about 30 minutes. Serves 6.

# Le Fleur's

This restaurant specializes in a small but excellent menu of seafoods and prime meats. There is a charming enclosed garden with a pool, for outdoor dining. Open every day for breakfast, lunch and dinner. It is in the Jacksonian Master Hosts Inn, on I-55 North in Jackson, Mississippi.

### GRASSHOPPER PIE

*Crust:* Combine 1¼ cups crushed chocolate wafers (save 2 tbsp. to sprinkle on top) with 4 tbsp. melted butter. Press into 9-inch pie tin evenly. Put in freezer for 1 hour.

*Filling:* Combine 17 large marshmallows and 7 tbsp. cream in a heavy pan. Heat slowly, stir until marshmallows are melted. When mixture is cool, whip 6 oz. whipping cream; fold into marshmallow mixture. Then add 2 tbsp. white crème de cacao and 2 tbsp. green crème de menthe.

Mix well and pour into pie shell. Sprinkle top with 2 tbsp. crushed chocolate wafers. Return to freezer for at least 2 hours. If frozen overnight, pie should be partially thawed before serving.

Left: Le Fleur's, Jacksonian Master Hosts Inn, Jackson, Mississippi (painting by Don Smith); lower left: Tiak O'Khata Restaurant, Louisville, Mississippi (painting by Robert Taylor); below: Mendenhall Hotel, Mendenhall, Mississippi (painting by Robert Taylor)

# Sheraton Rex Plaza

The Terrace Room in this modern lodge in Tupelo, Mississippi, offers fine food in elegant surroundings. Open for breakfast, lunch and dinner daily. It is on U.S. 45 and 70, not far from Natchez Trace National Parkway.

## SHORT RIBS OF BEEF MANDARIN

5 lb. short ribs of beef     1 tbsp. beef base
½ cup chopped green pepper
½ cup chopped onion     ½ tbsp. garlic salt
2 tbsp. butter
Flour to make thick base
1 tbsp. soy sauce     ½ cup red wine

Place short ribs in a large pan; add beef base, cover with water and cook in a 500° oven until brown; remove from oven and dip fat from the broth. Sauté pepper and onion in butter until tender, add flour, some of the stock from the beef ribs and cook until it forms a gravy, then add garlic salt, soy sauce and wine. Pour over short ribs and put back in oven for 25 to 30 minutes. Serve in casserole. Makes 8 portions.

## SHRIMP SALAD, REMOULADE SAUCE

Combine 2 cups mayonnaise with ½ cup Louisiana hot mustard (or to taste), 2 tbsp. horseradish, ½ small onion, grated, 1 hard-boiled egg, grated, and 2 tbsp. grated dill pickle. Mix well.

Arrange 3 lb. cleaned and cooked shrimp on a bed of lettuce and serve with sauce. Serves 6.

# Plaza III

This handsome restaurant is located next to the floodlighted fountain at the corner of Ward Parkway and Penn at the Country Club Plaza in Kansas City, Missouri. There are 6 completely separate dining areas, reflecting true Spanish-Mexican décor. Entire wood panels, ornate doors, wooden beams and wrought-iron decorations were brought from Mexico to create an atmosphere of elegance and beauty. Open Monday through Friday, 11:30 a.m. to 11 p.m.; Saturday, 11:30 a.m. to midnight; Sunday, 5 to 10 p.m. Closed on some holidays.

## PLAZA III STEAK SOUP

1 cup ground beef     1 cup flour
1 stick butter or margarine
5 cups water     1 tsp. Ac'cent (MSG)
½ tsp. black pepper     1 tbsp. beef base
18 oz. can tomatoes, chopped
1½ tsp. Kitchen Bouquet
½ cup each of chopped onions, carrots and celery, parboiled
1 cup frozen mixed vegetables

Brown meat and drain. Melt butter in a 2-quart pan and whip in flour to make a smooth paste. Add water and stir while heating to thicken, continue stirring. Add Ac'cent, pepper, beef base, tomatoes, and cook a minute. Add Kitchen Bouquet, rest of vegetables and cooked beef. Cook over medium heat for 30 minutes, stirring occasionally. *Do not salt.* Makes 1½ quarts and may be frozen for later use.

# Putsch's 210

This elegant dining room is in the Country Club Shopping Plaza, at 210 West 47th Street (U.S. 50), Kansas City, Missouri. Open for lunch, dinner and late supper except Sunday. A string trio provides dinner music. Reservations desirable.

## RAW SPINACH SALAD

½ cup celery and ½ cup onions, chopped fine
3 hard-boiled eggs, chopped
¾ cup Old English cheese, cubed
4 cups raw spinach, chopped     ½ tsp. salt
½ tsp. Tabasco     1½ tsp. vinegar
1½ cups mayonnaise     10 lettuce cups
10 tsp. horseradish

Combine celery, onions, eggs and cheese. Mix with spinach, tossing lightly. Combine salt, Tabasco, vinegar, mayonnaise; add to spinach mixture and fold lightly. Place salad in 10 lettuce cups, garnish each with 1 tsp. of horseradish on the side. Makes 10 portions.

## STUFFED CLAMS

1 onion, minced     ¼ lb. butter
1 cup flour     2 cups clam liquid
4 cups chopped clams     Salt and pepper
¼ cup sherry     ¼ cup sauterne

Sauté onions in butter, add flour and let cook a few minutes. Heat clam liquid and add to flour mixture. Add clams, remaining liquid, salt and pepper to taste, and wines. Place in serving shells, sprinkle with paprika, and brown lightly in hot oven. Serves 10.

Top: Sheraton Rex Plaza, Tupelo, Mississippi (painting
by Eldon Collier); center:
Plaza III, Kansas City, Missouri (painting by Don Whitney); right: Putsch's 210,
Kansas City, Missouri (illustration by Joan Solmes)

# Pope's Round Table Restaurant

Its comfortable atmosphere, fine food, and famous nut torte dessert make this restaurant one of the city's most popular. Lunch and dinner served year-round except Christmas Day. This restaurant is at Lindbergh and Lemay Ferry Road in Mehlville, Missouri (St. Louis area), near the South County Shopping Center.

## NUT TORTE

Beat 4 room-temperature egg whites with ⅛ tsp. cream of tartar until whites form *soft* peaks. Sift together ½ cup white sugar and ½ cup brown sugar, firmly packed, then add slowly to whites, beating after each addition until whites are stiff and glossy. Thoroughly mix in 1 tsp. vanilla and ¼ tsp. almond extract.

Combine ¾ cup finely crushed graham cracker crumbs and 2 tbsp. pecan pieces and sprinkle a little at a time over egg whites, folding in gently after each addition. Place batter in heavily greased 8-inch cake pan (2 inches deep), bake in preheated 300° oven for 30 minutes. Torte will be light in color when done. Cool in pan.

Arrange 1½ bananas, sliced in ⅛ inch slices, on top of cooled torte which has been removed from pan. Whip 1 cup whipping cream and decorate top and sides of torte. Garnish with 2 tbsp. of slivered toasted almonds or pecans and maraschino cherries. Refrigerate until served. Makes 8 portions.

# Tony's

Vincent and Anthony Bommarito are the owners of this elegant Italian restaurant at 826 North Broadway at King Drive in the historic old section of downtown St. Louis, Missouri. Dinner served from 5 p.m. to midnight every day, except Sunday and Monday. Reservations are not taken.

## TAGLIATELLE WITH CLAM SAUCE

4 dozen littleneck clams
1 clove garlic, chopped      ¼ cup olive oil
¼ cup chopped parsley
1 lb. tagliatelle or pasta of your choice
1 tsp. freshly ground pepper

Steam clams, remove from the shell, chop and set aside. Sauté garlic in olive oil with parsley. Add clams to oil and parsley. Cook pasta, drain and add to the clam mixture. Add pepper. Toss, remove from fire immediately and serve on preheated platters with a salad of crisp romaine leaves and chilled Soave or Frascati wine.

# Cellar Restaurant

Located at Hightower, a fine specialty store in downtown Oklahoma City, Oklahoma, the Cellar is noted for its handsome décor and excellent cuisine. Open for lunch only, 11:30 a.m. to 2:30 p.m., Monday through Friday. The address is 105 North Hudson Street, 3 blocks north of I-40.

## MOUSSE AU CHOCOLAT

15 oz. German's Sweet Chocolate
¼ lb. unsalted butter      1 cup sugar
⅜ cup white corn syrup      ¼ cup water
½ cup egg yolks      1 cup egg whites
1½ cups whipping cream, whipped until stiff
Chopped pistachio nuts (optional)

Place the chocolate and butter in a double boiler and melt. Make a syrup by combining the sugar, syrup and water and cooking until it will spin an 8-inch thread (234°). There should be about ½ cup syrup.

Beat the egg yolks until thick and lemony, slowly pour the hot syrup into the egg yolks and continue beating. Add cooled, melted chocolate to the above mixture. Beat the egg whites to stiff peaks, fold into chocolate mixture. Place in stainless steel bowl and allow to set overnight in refrigerator.

Remove chocolate mixture from refrigerator (it will now be very stiff). Place chocolate in bowl with 1 cup heavy cream, whipped, and beat furiously until it is a fluffy, creamy mass of rich chocolate. Decorate with the remaining whipped cream and garnish with the chopped pistachio nuts. Serves 12 to 15.

Top: Pope's Round Table Restaurant, Oklahoma City, Oklahoma (painting by Howard Whims); left: Tony's, St. Louis, Missouri (painting by Phil Austin); lower left; Cellar Restaurant, Oklahoma City, Oklahoma (painting by Jay O'Meilia)

# Dolores Restaurant

Three blocks west of the State Capitol, this landmark restaurant is conveniently located at 33 Northeast 23rd Street, Oklahoma City, Oklahoma. For over 42 years the same owners have served excellent food in a friendly atmosphere. Open 11 a.m. to 9:45 p.m. daily. Closed Thanksgiving and Christmas Day.

### BLACK BOTTOM PIE

Add 4 egg yolks to 2 cups scalded milk. Combine ½ cup of sugar with 1¼ tbsp. cornstarch and stir into milk. Cook in double boiler for 20 minutes, stirring occasionally until mixture generously coats a spoon.

Remove custard from heat and take out 1 cupful. Add 1½ squares unsweetened, melted chocolate to the cup of custard and beat well. When chocolate custard cools add 1 tsp. vanilla, then pour into a 9-inch baked gingersnap crust.

Blend 1 tsbp. gelatin with 4 tbsp. cold water and add to remaining hot custard. Let it cool but not thicken.

Beat 4 egg whites, ½ cup sugar and ½ tsp. cream of tartar into a meringue and fold into cool custard. Add 2 tbsp. rum. As soon as chocolate custard has set, pour this mixture over it. Chill again until set. Whip 1 cup whipping cream and spread on top of pie. Shave 1 square of bitter chocolate over pie and serve.

### PECAN PIE

1 cup white Karo syrup      1 cup sugar
3 beaten eggs      3 tbsp. melted butter
1 cup pecan halves      9-inch unbaked pie shell

Mix Karo syrup and sugar together. Add beaten eggs and melted butter and mix thoroughly. Scatter pecan halves on bottom of pie shell, then pour in filling. Bake at 300° for first 15 minutes, then bake until done at 275°, about 30 to 45 minutes.

# Spanish Village

Guadalupe Abeita's grandmother once lived in a part of the old building which houses his restaurant today. The Spanish Village is popular with diners who enjoy food with a Spanish accent. Open daily, 10 a.m. to 11 p.m.; closed on Wednesday. It is in downtown Austin, Texas, at 802 Red River Street.

### CHILES RELLENOS

1 lb. ground round steak
2 slices soft bread soaked in ½ cup milk
½ cup raisins      ½ cup ground pecans
¼ tsp. cloves      ¼ tsp. cinnamon
½ tsp. salt      4 slices Velveeta cheese
4 green peppers, hollowed

Mix ground round steak thoroughly with bread, raisins, pecans, and seasonings. Stuff peppers with this mixture and stand upright in baking dish covered with Spanish Sauce (below). Bake in 350° oven for an hour. About 10 minutes before serving top each pepper with a slice of cheese. Serves 4.

*Spanish Sauce:* Combine 1 cup tomato purée, ½ cup water, 1 chopped onion, 1 chopped green pepper, 1 tsp. salt, ½ tsp. pepper. Cook 20 to 25 minutes, stirring frequently.

### BURRITOS VILLA ESPAÑOLA

5 lb. chuck beef cut in 1-inch pieces
2 tbsp. salt      1 cup chopped green pepper
1¾ tbsp. cumin      1½ fresh tomatoes, chopped
1½ tbsp. garlic powder      1 cup chopped celery
3½ cups stewed tomatoes
½ medium onion, chopped

Brown meat with salt, cumin, garlic and onion. Then add rest of ingredients. Cook until tender, about 1 hour. Can be served over rice or wrapped in a flour tortilla, with hot sauce on the side. Serves 10 to 12.

Above: Dolores Res-
taurant, Oklahoma
City, Oklahoma (paint-
ing by Jay O'Meilia);
right: Spanish Village,
Austin, Texas (painting
by Ralph White)

# Las Columnas

This elegant dining room, which captures the mood of the sun-drenched Mediterranean, is in the Marriott Motor Hotel, 2101 Stemmons Freeway, just minutes from downtown Dallas. The dining room, one of several at the hotel, is open for lunch and dinner daily. Closed Sunday. Overnight accommodations and vacation facilities available at the hotel. Reservations advisable.

### SCAMPI BARCELONA

24 extra-large red prawns (or jumbo shrimp)
2 cups vegetable oil     1 tbsp. paprika
1 clove garlic, chopped fine
Juice of ½ lemon     Salt and pepper, to taste
½ lb. garlic butter     Chopped chives or parsley
12 oz. cooked flat noodles

Prepare a marinade of the vegetable oil, paprika, chopped garlic, lemon juice, and salt and pepper. Marinate the cleaned red prawns from 6 to 8 hours. Drain.

Sauté drained prawns in garlic butter (below) until done, then sauté cooked noodles in garlic butter.

Place a serving of noodles in the center of each plate and arrange 6 prawns around the noodles. Sprinkle lightly with parsley or chopped chives. Makes 4 portions. Serve with large spears of fresh broccoli as companion dish.

*Garlic Butter:* Combine ½ lb. melted butter with 1 chopped garlic clove.

# Los Troncos Restaurant

Victor Sears built his unique restaurant in Houston out of native Texas trees. Located at 1516 Westheimer, the Los Troncos (Tree House) Restaurant took 3 years to build and is constructed of trees and tree parts measuring up to 22 feet and weighing up to 5 tons. Diners must climb special log spiral stairways, cross over hand-hewn oak bridges, duck rough beams and even crawl into some of the seats. Open from 6 to 10:30 p.m. Monday through Thursday; Friday and Saturday to midnight. Closed Sunday. Reservations advisable.

### HUACHINANGO Â LA VERACRUZANA

1 cleaned whole red snapper (about 4½ lb.)
2 cloves garlic     4 tbsp. olive oil
3 onions, sliced     6 tomatoes, sliced
½ cup stuffed olives, sliced
Chopped parsley     2 chiles amarillos
Lemon juice, salt and pepper to taste

Brown garlic cloves in hot oil and then remove garlic. Fry onion slices in the oil until browned. Add tomatoes, olives, chopped parsley, lemon juice, salt and pepper. Cook slightly and pour over fish. Arrange chile strips on top. Bake in 350° oven until fish flakes. Garnish with lemon wedges. Serves 6.

# Massa's Restaurant

Tony Massa has been host to discriminating diners in Houston for over 20 years. His restaurant is noted not only for its national-award winning design, but for excellent seafood specialties. It is in the heart of the city at 802 Rusk Avenue, and is open for lunch and dinner daily except Sunday.

Free parking at the Bank of Texas garage next door after 5 p.m. Massa's is open from 11 a.m. to 11 p.m.

### MASSA'S SEAFOOD GUMBO

4 tbsp. flour     ½ cup cooking oil
1 tbsp. finely chopped garlic     1 quart water
1 cup each diced onions and celery
½ pint fresh oysters     ½ tsp. pepper
½ pint peeled, cleaned shrimp     1 tsp. salt
1 tsp. Spice Islands gumbo filé
2 cups cooked rice

Put oil in skillet, add flour, stir until dark brown. Add garlic, onions and celery and sauté.

In another pot bring water to a boil. Add first mixture and simmer for 45 minutes. Then add oysters, shrimp, salt and pepper, and cook for 10 minutes. Add filé. (This mixture of ground sassafras and thyme thickens the sauce and gives a distinctive Creole flavor.) Serve over rice. Makes 4 portions.

Top: Las Columnas, Dallas, Texas (painting by Adele Bichan); above: Los Troncos Restaurant, Houston, Texas (painting by Bob Rozas); right: Massa's Restaurant, Houston, Texas (painting by Mark Storm)

## Savoy Room,
## Houston Oaks Hotel

Located in the Houston Oaks Hotel in Houston's new Galleria Mall, just a block from I-610, the Savoy Room is done in elegant Georgian décor with warm cherrywood paneling and clusters of hunting and country scenes. Lunch is served Monday through Friday; dinner served every night. Reservations recommended.

### PINEAPPLE AND BANANA FLAMBÉ

Cut stalks and ends from whole pineapple. Turn upside down and trim sides. Quarter and remove center core. Split pieces in half again.

Place 6 oz. butter in a flambé pan and melt. Add 2 tsp. sugar and brown lightly. Peel 4 bananas and split in half. Add banana and pineapple to pan. Glaze lightly. Add juice from 1 lemon and 1 orange and 4 oz. banana liqueur. Flame with 2 oz. cherry brandy. Place fruits around 4 scoops of coffee ice cream and pour 1 oz. Kahlua over them. Makes 4 portions.

### STEAK DIANE FLAMBÉ AU COGNAC

Melt 4 oz. sweet butter in flambé pan. Put four 10-oz. New York steaks in the hot butter, season with salt and pepper, to taste. Sauté steaks on both sides until golden brown.

Add 4 tbsp. sliced fresh mushrooms and 2 tbsp. chopped shallots. Sauté them. Add 5 oz. cognac to the flambé pan. Remove steaks, add 2 cups heated burgundy and 2 tsp. chopped parsley. Serve sauce over steaks.

### DOVER SOLE A LA MEUNIÈRE

4 whole Dover sole (18 oz. each)
Juice of 2 lemons
1 tbsp. Worcestershire Sauce    Salt and pepper
1 cup flour    Oil for frying
12 oz. butter    2 tsp. chopped parsley

Clean sole, remove skin and fins. Pour lemon juice, Worcestershire Sauce, salt and pepper over sole and marinate for 5 minutes. Flour lightly and fry in oil to a golden brown. Place in a 350° oven for 3 minutes.

Brown butter in a separate pan, add a little lemon juice and parsley. Serve separately.

## Barth's Restaurant

For over 40 years a combination of delicious food and friendly atmosphere has made this restaurant on U.S. 181 in Kenedy, Texas, popular with tourists and residents alike. Open daily from 5:30 a.m. to 10 p.m. Reservations not necessary. Closed on Christmas Day. Mr. and Mrs. James W. Nichols are the owners. Mrs. Madelyn Sims is the manager.

### PECAN PIE

2 cups dark Karo syrup
2 tbsp. melted butter
½ tsp. nutmeg    ½ tsp salt
1 tbsp. flour    3 eggs
9-inch unbaked pie shell
½ cup pecans

Add syrup to butter. Combine nutmeg, salt and flour. Add to first mixture and stir well. Beat eggs and fold into mixture. Pour into pie shell. Bake in 350° oven about 15 minutes. Cover pie with layer of chopped pecans.

## Sheraton-Fairway
## Motor Hotel

The beautiful Rio Grande Valley, an all-year vacation land of palm trees and tropical flowers, is the setting for this modern motel and restaurant in McAllen, Texas. It has 3 swimming pools and a putting green, with 2 golf courses nearby. The restaurant is open from 6:30 a.m. to 10 p.m. every day all year. The Sheraton-Fairway is on State Highway 336, half a mile south of U.S. 83.

### WESTERN CHILI CASSEROLE

1½ lb. ground beef    1 cup chopped onion
¼ cup chopped celery    ¼ tsp. pepper
15-oz. can chili con carne with beans
2 cups corn chips, slightly crushed
1 cup shredded sharp cheese

Brown meat, then add celery and ¾ cup of the onion; cook till just tender. Drain off excess fat. Add chili and pepper, heat.

Place layer of chips in ungreased 1½-quart casserole. Alternate layers of chili mixture, chips and cheese (reserve ¼ cup of the cheese and some of the onion for topping).

On the top in the center, sprinkle remaining onion and cheese. Cover and bake in 350° oven for 10 minutes or until heated through. Before serving, border casserole with corn chips. Serves 6.

Top: Savoy Room, Houston Oaks Hotel, Houston, Texas (painting by Bob Rozas); left: Barth's Restaurant, Kenedy, Texas (painting by Warren Hunter); below: Sheraton-Fairway Motor Hotel, Mc-Allen, Texas (painting by Mark Storm).

# Charles V

French-American cuisine is offered at this elegant, intimate dining room in the St. Anthony Hotel at 300 East Travis Street in downtown San Antonio. Open every day except Sunday. Lunch served 11:30 a.m. to 2:30 p.m. and dinner from 5:30 p.m. to 9:30 p.m. Reservations advisable. Overnight accommodations at the hotel.

## SPINACH PUDDING

2 cups cooked spinach, chopped very fine
2 tbsp. melted butter        3 eggs, beaten
1 cup light cream        ½ tsp. salt
⅛ tsp. pepper        Few drops of onion juice
3 tbsp. soft butter        2 cups fine bread crumbs

Combine all ingredients except soft butter and bread crumbs. Take a clean dish towel and spread with soft butter, forming a 9- to 10-inch square. Sprinkle with crumbs.

Cover crumbed area with spinach mixture and form into a roll about 1½ inches thick. Tie ends and middle loosely with string. Put in a flat pan and steam 30 minutes. When done, remove towel and glaze with additional melted butter. Cut roll into 12 slices before serving.

# Earl Abel's

"A million a year eat here" is the boast of this popular 37-year-old family restaurant which is open 24 hours day. It is 4 miles north of the downtown area of San Antonio at 4200 Broadway (Business Route U.S. 81), and it is owned by Mrs. Earl Abel.

## TURKEY MORNAY

7 tbsp. melted butter or margarine
7 tbsp. flour        ½ pint scalded milk
½ lb. mild Cheddar cheese, grated
12 thick, cooked turkey slices        6 pieces toast

Melt butter or margarine, blend in flour and cook for 2 minutes. Add scalded milk and grated cheese, beat until creamy and smooth. Place turkey on toast slices. Cover with cheese sauce and bake in 375° oven until golden brown. Serves 6.

## PLANKED CHOPPED SIRLOIN STEAK

Thoroughly mix 2 lb. ground sirloin with salt and pepper. Shape into 4 patties. Slice 1 large tomato and 1 jumbo white onion in ¼-inch slices. Cook patties until done as desired. Sauté onion rings until golden and when they are done heat tomato slices, being careful not to overheat.

Place an onion slice and tomato slice on top of each cooked pattie and arrange patties on 4 oak planks. Decorate the border of the planks with 3 cups of mashed potatoes squeezed through a pastry bag. Heat under broiler until tips of potatoes are golden brown. Serve immediately. Makes 4 portions.

# La Louisiane

This restaurant was founded in 1935 by Max Manus, who still operates it. He is dedicated to serving the finest food available, with personalized service in a quiet, relaxed atmosphere. Lunch served noon to 2 p.m.; dinner 5:30 to 10 p.m. Closed on Sundays and from August 24 to September 7. It is located on U.S. 81 at 2632 Broadway, in San Antonio, 1 mile north of the downtown area.

## CHICKEN SAUTÉ

Use only the breasts and legs from two 3-lb. chickens. Remove the bones. Dip chicken lightly in flour and place in frying pan with melted butter. Sauté chicken in covered pan until brown on all sides (about 20 minutes). Separately prepare ¼ lb. wild rice according to directions on package.

In another frying pan place 2 tbsp. melted butter; 12 hearts of artichoke; 12 fresh mushrooms, sliced; 1 oz. sherry; 1 tsp. lemon juice; 4 tbsp. Escoffier Sauce (or other good meat sauce) and salt and pepper to taste.

Cook mixture until artichoke hearts and mushrooms are done and ingredients well-blended (about 10 minutes). Place the hot wild rice in a serving dish, top with chicken pieces. Spoon artichoke-mushroom mixture over all. Serves 4.

Top: Charles V, St. Anthony Hotel, San Antonio, Texas (painting by Warren Hunter); above: Earl Abel's, San Antonio, Texas (illustration by Rudy Laslo); right: La Louisiane, San Antonio, Texas (painting by Mark Storm)

## Luby's Cafeteria

This is one of a chain of popular cafeterias noted for their excellent variety of foods and their own pastries. This one is in downtown San Antonio at 4902 Broadway. Lunch and dinner served daily, lunch from 11 a.m. to 2 p.m. and dinner from 4:30 to 8 p.m.

### CARROT CAKE

Into mixing bowl sift together and mix well:

2⅓ cups cake flour, or 2 cups plus
1 tbsp. regular flour
2 cups granulated sugar      1 tsp. baking soda
2 tsp. baking powder      1 tsp. salt
2 tsp. ground cinnamon

Add 1¼ cups salad oil. Beat for 2 minutes, starting at medium speed and increasing to fast. Scrape down sides of bowl while mixing. Add 4 eggs and 2 tsp. vanilla extract; beat for 2 more minutes, scraping down sides. Stir in 2 cups finely grated carrots, 1 cup drained crushed pineapple and 1 cup chopped pecans.

Pour into two 9-inch or three 7- or 8-inch greased and floured cake pans. Bake at 325° for 45 to 50 minutes. Remove from oven, cool for 15 minutes, then turn out on cake rack.

*Frosting:* Soften 6 oz. cream cheese in 3 tbsp. cream and 1½ tsp. vanilla. Beat for 5 to 7 minutes or until light and fluffy. Add ½ tsp. salt, then 1 lb. confectioners' sugar, one cup at a time, blending well after each addition. Stir in ¾ cup pecans, ½ cup raisins, ½ cup coconut.

## The Stockman

Twenty-two San Antonio businessmen recently decided to open a restaurant which would also serve as a museum of the cattle industry. The result is The Stockman, a stunning new restaurant which appropriately is housed in a historic riverfront building (409 East Commerce) where for a century expert leather craftsmen turned out saddles and bridles. Lunch and dinner served Monday through Friday; dinner only on Saturday and Sunday. Reservations necessary.

### STUFFED ARTICHOKES

6 fresh artichokes      2 quarts boiling water
Freshly squeezed lemon juice
2 tsp. salt      ½ cup olive oil
1 cup chopped mushrooms
2 cloves garlic, crushed      1 small onion, minced
½ cup melted butter      ¼ cup chopped parsley
½ lb. ground cooked ham      2 cups bread crumbs
1 cup grated Parmesan cheese

Cut tips from artichokes and brush with lemon juice. Cook until tender in boiling water, to which salt and olive oil have been added. Drain artichokes and remove centers.

Sauté mushrooms, garlic, and onion in butter until browned. Stir in parsley, ham, cheese and bread crumbs and mix well. Spoon into artichoke shells and heat at 325° about 15 minutes. Serve hot. Serves 6.

## The Kangaroo Court

Guests can board a river boat in front of the patio of this restaurant which is on the Paseo del Rio, a section of the San Antonio River, in San Antonio. It is just a block from the Alamo and the old Spanish section. The address is 316 North Presa Street. Lunch and dinner served daily.

### CHEESE CAKE

*Crust:* Mix 2½ cups graham cracker crumbs with 3 oz. melted butter and 2 tbsp. sugar. Press into bottom and sides of a 10 x 2½-inch spring form cheese cake pan.

*Filling:*

4 large eggs, beaten      1 cup sugar
3 tsp. vanilla      16 oz. sour cream
24 oz. cream cheese, cut up

Beat sugar and vanilla into beaten eggs. Add pieces of cream cheese, a little at a time. Beat mixture 15 minutes at high speed in a mixer. Fold in sour cream. Pour into graham crust and bake 35 to 45 minutes at 350°.

*Topping:* Mix 16 oz. sour cream with 2 tsp. vanilla and 2 tbsp. sugar. Place on top of cooled cheesecake and put into 450° oven for 10 minutes. Remove from oven. Refrigerate cake for at least 8 hours before serving. Fresh strawberries, blueberries or raspberries may be added. Serves 8 to 12.

Top: The Kangaroo Court, San Antonio, Texas (painting by Konrad Kahl); lower left: The Stockman, San Antonio, Texas (photo by Bud Shannon); below: Luby's Cafeteria, San Antonio, Texas (illustration by Ed Paulson)

# West

Blessed with an abundance of native fruits, seafood and meat, Western chefs have nevertheless always augmented their regional menus with dishes from "back home." Thus the homesick traveler from New England will find a Vermont Christmas goose, and the nostalgic Texan a chicken mole, along with the West's own distinctive foods. Some of these are shown in this still life, with Rex Brandt's Southern California landscape as backdrop.

# Fairbanks Inn

Informality with luxury awaits guests at this motor hotel conveniently located at 1521 Cushman where it crosses 15th Street (the Alaska Highway) in downtown Fairbanks, Alaska. Breakfast, lunch and dinner served daily. Dining room open until midnight. Among nearby tourist attractions are the gold dredges and the University of Alaska Museum.

## HUSKY KING CRAB BOAT

1 lb. fresh-frozen Alaska king crabmeat
1 green pepper, diced     1 oz. onion, diced
3 oz. sherry wine     2 oz. pimento, diced
1 pint white cream sauce
2 cups whipped potatoes
4 hard-boiled eggs, shredded

Simmer green pepper and onion in sherry until tender. Drain. Add pepper, onion, pimento and wine to heated cream sauce. Heat crabmeat in salted water. Prepare 4 individual oblong casseroles, with a rosette of potatoes in each end, or 1 large casserole with potatoes at edge.

Spoon 3 oz. of sauce into each, then drain crabmeat and place equal portions on top of sauce. Sprinkle each serving with shredded eggs. Serves 4.

# Francisco Grande Hotel

Baseball is a favorite conversational topic at this 9-story Arizona hotel because the nearby town of Casa Grande is the spring training grounds of the San Francisco Giants and their farm clubs. There are even bat-and-ball-shaped swimming pools here, as well as an 18-hole championship golf course and excellent family vacation facilities. The dining rooms are open every day from 7 a.m. to 11 p.m. The hotel is on State Highway 84, midway between Phoenix and Tucson, 4 miles west of Casa Grande.

## DOVE OR QUAIL WITH RICE DRESSING

Wash and dry 16 to 20 cleaned birds. Rub with salt and flour and sauté lightly in butter. Place in roasting pan. Then lightly sauté ¼ cup finely chopped onion, ½ cup finely chopped mushrooms and 1 tbsp. chopped parsley. Combine with ½ cup of white wine and pour over birds. Cover pan and roast at 375° until tender. Serve with rice dressing (above). Serves 15.

## RICE DRESSING

2 cups Uncle Ben's converted rice
3 large onions     4 stalks celery
1 green pepper     Giblets of 4 birds
½ cup butter     1 tbsp. salt
1 tbsp. poultry seasoning     2 eggs
1 cup chopped pecans     ½ cup chopped parsley
Mushooms (optional)

Cook rice as directed on package. Grind giblets. Chop onions, celery and pepper fine; then combine with ground giblets and sauté in butter until thoroughly cooked. Add seasonings.

Beat eggs until frothy. Combine onion mixture with rice, then fold in beaten eggs. Add chopped nuts and parsley, and mushrooms if desired. Bake in shallow greased casserole 25 minutes at 350°. (This is also good with chicken or turkey.)

# El Chorro Lodge

Nestled in a valley between Camelback and Mummy mountains on the sun-drenched desert, this popular restaurant is owned and operated by Janet and Mark Gruber. Open November 1 to May 1, serving breakfast, lunch and dinner daily. Overnight accommodations. Reservations necessary. The address is 5550 East Lincoln Drive, Phoenix, Arizona.

## STRAWBERRY CHANTILLY

Rub strawberries through a sieve to make 1 cup purée. Add 12 tbsp. sugar and a pinch of salt. Soak 1½ tsp. gelatin in 2 tbsp. water. Dissolve over hot water and add to strawberry purée. Beat 2 cups whipping cream until stiff and fold into the strawberry mixture.

Put 1 meringue layer (below) in ice cube tray. Cover with half of strawberry mixture. Top with meringue and freeze. Make a second freezer tray of dessert with remaining meringue and strawberry mixture. Serve in squares topped with whipped cream and strawberries. Serves 16.

*Meringue Layers:* Beat 4 egg whites until stiff. Add ¾ cup sugar gradually and ¼ tsp. vanilla. Fold in 5½ tsp. sugar and shape on tin sheet covered with letter paper in 4 portions the size of freezer tray. Bake about 30 minutes at 250°. Turn over and remove paper by laying a damp cloth over it for a few minutes.

Above: Fairbanks Inn, Fairbanks, Alaska (painting by Frank D. Hagel); right: Francisco Grande Hotel, Casa Grande, Arizona (painting by Francis Beaugureau); below: El Chorro Lodge, Phoenix, Arizona (painting by William Schimmel)

# Arizona Inn

This truly luxurious resort hotel in Tucson, Arizona, is located at 2200 East Elm Street, 3 miles east of downtown. Breakfast, lunch and dinner served daily. Sunday night buffet supper served from 6:30 to 8:15 p.m., and during January, February and March a daily buffet luncheon is served from 1 to 2:30 p.m. Reservations advisable. Open all year.

### CURRIED FRUIT

| | |
|---|---|
| 14-oz. can sliced pineapple | 14-oz. can pears |
| 14-oz. can peaches | 2 tbsp. cornstarch |
| 1½ cups combined pineapple and pear juice | |
| ¾ stick butter | 4 tsp. curry powder |
| ½ cup brown sugar | ½ lemon, juice |

Arrange drained fruit in casserole. Add cornstarch to fruit juice. Cook until clear and somewhat thickened. Add butter.

Mix curry powder and brown sugar, pour hot sauce over mixture and stir until sugar melts. Add lemon juice. Pour over fruit. Bake 1 hour at 350°. Put in refrigerator overnight.

Heat about 45 minutes before serving. Delightful by itself, as a relish, and particularly good served over vanilla ice cream. Serves 8.

# Amelia's Restaurant

Amelia, born on the Isle of Capri, is the owner and cook at this friendly restaurant where she likes to work with an open door to the dining room. At 311 Marine Avenue on Balboa Island in California (adjacent to Newport Beach), the restaurant serves dinner every day except Monday. Reservations necessary. Closed in November.

### AMELIA'S LADY SOLE

Beat 1 egg and combine with 1 cup milk. Dip 12 sole fillets in this mixture, then in 1½ cups of fine bread crumbs. Arrange 18 chopped scallops on 6 of the fillets, top with butter. Broil all fillets for 5 minutes or bake in a 350° oven for 12 minutes.

Place plain fillets on those covered with scallops. Melt ½ cup butter in saucepan and stir in ½ cup flour to make a smooth paste. Mix in 1 cup small sliced sautéed mushrooms and 1½ cups cooked shredded Alaskan king crab. Salt and pepper to taste. Add 1 cup

grated Cheddar cheese, 1 tbsp. chopped chives and 1 tbsp. chopped parsley; stir in 1 cup semidry sherry and cook into a smooth sauce by adding egg-and-milk mixture left over from dipping fillets. *Do not boil.* Pour sauce over layered sole and sprinkle with 4 tbsp. toasted, sliced almonds. Makes 6 portions.

# The Pot Luck

This pleasant gourmet restaurant reflects the taste and imagination of its owner and executive chef, Henry Rubin, who also is an expert, and writer, on the subject of wine.

It is housed in a modest 1894 building at 2400 San Pablo Avenue in Berkeley, California. From the East Shore Freeway take the University Exit and proceed a half mile east to San Pablo Avenue. Lunch served Monday through Friday from 11:30 a.m. to 2:30 p.m. Dinner is served every night in a relaxed candlelight atmosphere. Reservations recommended.

### BLACK MUSHROOM SOUP

Soak 1½ cups dried, smoked, black mushrooms overnight in cold water. Rinse, then boil in slightly salted water to cover until just tender. In a separate pan bring to a boil 3 quarts of strong chicken stock, then add ⅜ tsp. garlic powder, ¾ tsp. onion powder, ¾ cup chopped onions, and 2 stalks of celery, finely sliced. Simmer for half an hour.

Meanwhile drain mushrooms, saving the cooking water. Cut mushrooms into bite-size pieces and add to stock. Strain mushroom cooking water through a towel or cheesecloth; add to simmering stock. Cook 30 to 45 minutes. At the Pot Luck the soup is considered a meal and comes with thick slices of sourdough bread and butter.

### NAVY BEAN AND CABBAGE SOUP

Soak 1 lb. navy beans overnight. Next day, add water to cover, bring to a boil, reduce heat and simmer, covered, for 2½ hours.

Drain beans; combine with 3 quarts chicken stock, 1 lb. pork bones, 1 small chopped cabbage, 1½ cups chopped onion, 3 chopped carrots and 1 scant tsp. marjoram.

Simmer for 2½ hours. Remove and discard bones, and skim off surface fat. Season to taste with salt and pepper. Just before serving stir in ½ cup chopped parsley. Makes 3 quarts.

Top: Arizona Inn, Tucson, Arizona (painting by David Sorokin); above: Amelia's Restaurant, Balboa Island, California (painting by Ralph Hulett); right: The Pot Luck, Berkeley, California (painting by Louis Macouillard)

# Benbow Inn

An English Tudor mansion houses this resort hotel which is just 2 miles south of Garberville, on U.S. 101, in northern California. Breakfast, lunch and dinner served daily during the season—April 1 to November 1. Overnight accommodations and excellent vacation facilities. Reservations recommended June 15 to September 15.

### CHRISTMAS SUCKLING PIG

Select a suckling pig—the average weight is about 30 pounds. Clean and dry very well. Season interior with 2 tbsp. salt, 2 tsp. pepper and 1 tsp. nutmeg.

*Stuffing:* Chop pig liver very fine and sauté in butter for 5 minutes. Chop 2 medium-size onions and sauté in butter. Soak 1 loaf of dry bread in warm water for 15 minutes, then press out water and add the following:

| | |
|---|---|
| 3 eggs | 1 tbsp. salt |
| 2 tsp. pepper | 1 tbsp. sage |
| ½ tsp. nutmeg | ½ lb. sausage |
| 1 tbsp. chopped fresh parsley | |

Combine sautéed liver and onion with bread mixture and stuff pig. Sew opening very tightly and place on barbecue skewer. Turn slowly over hot coals for about 3 hours, baste frequently with drippings. Serve with gravy made from drippings. Serves 40 to 50.

*Alternate Method:* Place pig on large flat pan and roast in 350° oven for 6½ hours. Tuck legs under body and baste often.

# Scandia

Authentic Scandinavian decorations add to the elegance of this restaurant at 9040 Sunset Boulevard in Hollywood, California. It is open daily 11:30 a.m. to 1 a.m. for lunch, dinner and supper. On Sunday a special brunch is served from 11:30 a.m. to 3 p.m.

Reservations necessary. Closed on Mondays and Christmas Day.

### SCANDIA MEAT BALLS

| | |
|---|---|
| ½ lb. beef, ground twice | 1 tsp. salt |
| ½ lb. pork, ground twice | ¼ tsp. pepper |
| ½ cup fresh bread crumbs soaked in ½ cup milk | |
| ½ cup onions, chopped and sautéed in butter | |
| Pinch of allspice | 1 egg |
| ½ cup lukewarm milk | |
| ½ cup clarified butter or oil | 1 tbsp. flour |
| 1½ cups broth, consommé or milk | |

Combine all ingredients except lukewarm milk, clarified butter, flour and broth. Beat with wooden spoon, or on low speed of mixer, while slowly adding lukewarm milk. Allow mixture to stand in refrigerator until firm enough to roll into meat balls of walnut size.

Fry in skillet in butter or oil. When cooked through, drain off fat, dust meatballs lightly with flour, then pour in broth, consommé or milk and simmer for a few minutes. Serves 4 as entree, 8 to 10 as appetizer.

# Scotty Campbell's

This award-winning restaurant is a landmark of the San Francisco Bay area. It is famous for its prime beef and other delectable dishes served amid an interesting array of antiques. Open daily for dinner: Monday through Thursday 4:30 to 10:30 p.m.; Friday and Saturday 4:30 p.m. to 11 p.m. Sunday dinner 4 to 10 p.m. Reservations recommended on weekends and holidays. The address is 2907 El Camino Real in Redwood City, California. Take the Woodside Road-Harbor Boulevard turn-off from U.S. 101, go west to El Camino Real South Exit, then proceed for 5 blocks.

### PRIME RIB AS YOU LIKE IT

Order a 15-pound prime rib of beef with the fat cover left on. Lift flap and season with 2 tbsp. black pepper, 3 tbsp. Ac'cent (MSG) and 5 tbsp. salt. Close flap and tie with string 3 times around and once lengthwise. Place in pan fat side up and roast in 350° oven until meat thermometer registers 140°, about 4 hours. Do not use water in pan; roast prime ribs dry.

At the end of roasting time you will have a choice of medium, medium rare and rare. Serve with juice of meat or make gravy. Serves 10.

Top: Benbow Inn, Garberville, California (painting by Earl Thollander); above: Scandia, Hollywood, California (painting by Jake Lee); right: Scotty Campbell's, Redwood City, California (painting by Adele Bichan)

# The Firehouse

From 1853 to 1921 the building that houses this restaurant was a working firehouse. Today there are few traces of the old firehouse in the dining rooms, which are decorated with interesting antiques, or in the wine cellars and New Orleans-style courtyard. It is at 1112 Two Street (between K and L streets), in Sacramento, California. Open daily for dinner from 6 to 11 p.m. Closed Sunday. Reservations necessary.

### STEAK CARLO

2 filets of beef, 10 oz. each     2 tbsp. garlic oil
2 cups chopped shallots or mild onions
3 tsp. Worcestershire Sauce
5 tbsp. Escoffier Diable Sauce
5 tbsp. Escoffier Robert Sauce
2 tbsp. Escoffier Melba Sauce
4 whole sautéed mushrooms

Slice filets in half, butterfly style, removing all fat. Heat garlic oil in silver chafing dish, cook shallots until half done, add Worcestershire and the three Escoffier sauces. Simmer 5 minutes; add meat and cook 3 minutes on each side until medium rare. Cover with cooked sauce and top with mushrooms. Serves 4.

# Nena's Restaurant

The cozy atmosphere of an old-time Spanish mission pervades this fine eating place which serves typical Mexican fare as well as steaks. At 642 D Street in San Bernardino, it is open for lunch and dinner 7 days a week: Sunday through Thursday 11 a.m. to 10 p.m.; Friday and Saturday 11 a.m. to 11 p.m.

### GUACAMOLE DIP

3 ripe avocados    Tabasco Sauce, to taste
½ lemon, juice    Lettuce leaf
4 tbsp. sour cream    3 tomatoes, quartered
½ tsp. seasoned salt    Potato or corn chips

Mash avocados, then add lemon juice, sour cream and seasoned salt. Blend until creamy smooth. Add a few drops of Tabasco to taste for a spicy tangy flavor. Place dip on fresh crisp lettuce leaf cup and garnish with tomatoes. Provide chips for dipping. Makes 1 pint; serves 6 to 8.

# Anthony's Fish Grotto

Mrs. Catherine Ghio and her sons own and operate this beautiful San Diego restaurant which commands a dramatic view of the bay. At Harbor Drive and Ash Street, it is adjacent to the three-masted windjammer, *Star of India*, a popular tourist attraction. Lunch and dinner served every day except Tuesday. Reservations are accepted only for the Star of the Sea Room, which is open daily from 5 to 10 p.m.

### POACHED FISH DE PESCA

Boil 1 quart water in a deep, heavy pan. Place in it four 10-oz. pieces of whitefish (or halibut, snapper or salmon). Then add 2 medium-sized potatoes, peeled and cut in 1-inch slices; 2 bay leaves; 1 tsp. pickling spices; ¼ tsp. salt and ¼ tsp. Ac'cent (MSG). Simmer for 10 minutes.

Remove fish and potatoes to 4 individual casseroles (or 1 large shallow dish). Pour 3 oz. olive oil over all. Sprinkle with 1 tsp. chopped parsley, the juice of 1 lemon and freshly ground pepper. Serve with melted butter and 4 lemon halves wrapped in cheesecloth. Serves 4.

# Lubach's

This celebrated restaurant at 2101 North Harbor Drive on the San Diego waterfront displays the choicest selection of seafood in season, as well as the finest beef. Open for lunch and dinner daily; reservations necessary. Closed on Sundays and holidays.

### SHRIMP CABRILLO

Peel, clean and wash 36 large raw shrimp. On a skewer place 1 shrimp, 3 pieces of bacon, a piece of green pepper and a mushroom cap. Continue in this order until there are 6 shrimp on each of 6 skewers. Baste skewered shrimp with melted butter and season with salt and pepper to taste, then broil on both sides 8 inches from hot fire until shrimp are pink. Serve with sauce (below). Serves 6.

*Sauce Cabrillo:* Combine 1 tsp. Coleman mustard, 10 dashes Worcestershire Sauce, 5 dashes Tabasco and juice of ½ lemon. Add 14 oz. ketchup. Simmer for 20 minutes. Remove from fire, add 4 oz. butter a little at a time, using a wire whip.

Top: The Firehouse, Sacramento, California (painting by Norman Nicholson); left: Nena's Restaurant, San Bernardino, California (painting by Rex Brandt); lower left: Anthony's Fish Grotto, San Diego, California (painting by Rex Brandt); below: Lubach's, San Diego, California (painting by Rex Brandt)

# Empress of China

In a city noted for its excellent as well as handsome restaurants, this San Francisco establishment is outstanding. The décor is beautiful with a garden court and pavilion inspired by the Royal Park in Peking; there are magnificent antique chandeliers and brocaded jade green silk walls. Open for lunch and dinner every day; reservations necessary. It is at 838 Grant Avenue in Chinatown.

### EMPRESS BEEF

½ lb. sirloin of beef, cut into shoestring strips
3 tbsp. vegetable oil      1 scant tsp. salt
3 stalks celery, coarsely chopped
1 large white onion, sliced thin
1 small can button mushrooms, sliced
¼ lb. snow peas, fresh or frozen (if not available, substitute French-style green beans)
½ small can water chestnuts, coarsely chopped
1 tbsp.cornstarch      ½ tbsp. sugar
5 tbsp. soy sauce      ½ cup water
2 cups steamed rice

Brown beef in vegetable oil with salt in hot skillet. Add celery, onion, mushrooms, snow peas and water chestnuts. Stir slowly for a few minutes over hot fire. Then cover the pan, turn down fire and simmer for 3 minutes.

Just before serving stir in smooth combination of cornstarch, sugar, soy sauce and water. Serve immediately over mounds of hot rice. Serves 4.

# The Blue Fox

Located at 659 Merchant Street, a block from San Francisco's famous Chinatown, this restaurant is noted for its elegance and beauty as well as its excellent and unusual food. Dinner served 6 to 11 p.m. daily. Closed Sunday. Reservations are necessary. The Blue Fox is closed the last week in June and the first week in July.

### ZUCCHINI SOUFFLÉ

1 lb. zucchini      2 oz. butter
1 clove garlic, mashed
3 scallions, chopped fine
⅔ cup sauterne      Juice of ½ lemon
1 tbsp. chopped parsley
Pinch of nutmeg      Salt and pepper to taste
2 pimentos, diced fine
6 eggs, separated and beaten
2 tbsp. Parmesan cheese

Pare the tops and bottoms of the zucchini and cut it into strips about as big around as a pencil and about 1 inch long.

Heat butter in a skillet, add garlic and scallions, and sauté until half done. Add zucchini pieces and cook for 2 minutes, stirring several times.

Add sauterne, lemon juice, parsley, nutmeg and salt and pepper to taste. Cook briskly until the pan is almost dry and zucchini is tender but firm. Add pimentos, mix well. Remove from pan and put aside to cool.

In a bowl combine the beaten egg yolks with the Parmesan cheese. Add zucchini mixture and fold in stiffly beaten egg whites with a wooden spoon. Pour into a deep 2-quart baking dish which has been coated with butter and chilled. Place baking dish in a pan of cold water and bake in 400° oven for about 25 minutes, or until firm and fluffy. Serves 6.

# Del Vecchio's

Located at 1547 Meridian Road in the New Carriage Square Shopping Center in San Jose, California, this Victorian-style restaurant has a reputation for consistently good food. Lunch is served Monday through Friday; dinner served daily. Reservations necessary. John Gullotto and Louis Del Vecchio are the owners.

### FILET SAUTÉ MARSALA

16 slices of beef filet (1 oz. each)
2 oz. cooking oil      1 shallot, chopped fine
½ cup seasoned flour      1 cup sliced mushrooms
4 green onions, chopped
½ cup Marsala wine      Pinch of oregano
1 medium tomato, diced
¼ lemon      1 cup beef stock
Salt and pepper to taste

Heat oil in pan and sauté shallots until transparent. Dredge beef slices in seasoned flour and add to oil and shallots, cook on both sides until brown.

Add green onions and mushrooms, sauté until tender, drain off excess oil, return pan to fire and flame with the wine. Allow to cook about 1 minute or until ingredients absorb the liquid. Add oregano and diced tomatoes. Squeeze juice from lemon, add stock and cook gently until liquid barely covers meat. Salt and pepper to taste. Serves 4.

Top: Del Vecchio's, San Jose, California (painting by Michael W. Green); left: The Blue Fox, San Francisco, California (painting by Norman Nicholson); lower left: Empress of China, San Francisco, California (painting by Norman Nicholson)

# Malio's Restaurant

Diners have a double pleasure here: excellent seafood and a magnificent view of Monterey Bay. Malio's is on the picturesque municipal wharf in downtown Santa Cruz, California. Open every day from 11:30 a.m. to 11 p.m.; reservations advisable. Closed the first week in November.

### SOLE FLORENTINE

Roll up 18 fillets of sole (about 6 inches in length) and hold with toothpicks. Place rolls in square baking pan, cover with water, adding 1 tsp. salt, ½ tsp. white pepper, ¼ tsp. garlic salt, and 1 bay leaf. Poach in 450° oven for 15 to 20 minutes. Drain well and save 1 cup of liquid.

Cover the bottom of a large casserole with ½ lb. chopped cooked spinach. Arrange fillets in rows on spinach. Make a sauce by combining 1 cup poaching stock, 1 cup milk, ¼ cup dry sherry and 1 tbsp. Worcestershire Sauce with salt to taste. Bring to a boil. Thicken with 1 tbsp. cornstarch in equal amount of water. Pour sauce over fish rolls and sprinkle with ¾ cup grated Parmesan cheese. Brown in 450° oven for 8 to 10 minutes. Serves 6.

# Colonial Inn

This charming inn is on the old McNiel Ranch where the Wells Fargo Stage Coach stopped in the late 1800s to let weary travelers rest and enjoy a hearty meal. It is located in northern California in Trinidad, just off U.S. 101. The inn offers dinner only, from 5 to 10 p.m. (11 p.m. on Friday and Saturday) every weekday except Monday; on Sunday from 1 to 9 p.m. Closed January through March. Reservations accepted.

### SALAD CURRIED RICE WINSTON

| | |
|---|---|
| 3 cups raw rice | 1 tsp. salt |
| 1 tbsp. lemon juice | 1 dash yellow color |
| 1 lb. raw zucchini | 1 heaping tbsp. curry |
| 1 tsp. Ac'cent (MSG) | 1½ cups mayonnaise |
| 1 lb. bean sprouts | 4-oz. can water chestnuts |

Stir rice into 6½ cups boiling water. Add salt, lemon juice and yellow color. Bring to a rolling boil, reduce fire as low as possible, cover and cook 25 minutes. Remove from fire and allow to reach room temperature.

In the meantime, dice raw zucchini in approximately ¼-inch squares and add curry and Ac'cent to mayonnaise. Fold all ingredients into cooled rice. Serves 10 to 12.

# House of Garner

This excellent dining room is adjacent to the Ukiah Travelodge at 1090 South State Street in Ukiah, California. Take the Talmadge ramp from U.S. 101. Lunch and dinner served daily, with a smorgasbord every evening. Weekday and Sunday hours are 10 a.m. to 11 p.m. Closed most holidays and the first 2 weeks in January.

### TERIYAKI MARINADE

| | |
|---|---|
| 1½ cups pineapple juice | 2 bay leaves (small) |
| 4 tbsp. soy sauce | ¼ tsp. ground cloves |
| 4 tbsp. lemon juice | 3 tbsp. Liquid Smoke |
| 4 cloves garlic (pressed) | 1 tsp. grated ginger |

Combine all ingredients into a marinade for use with chicken or steak.

*For Chicken:* Cut young broilers or fryers into halves or quarters. Leave in marinade about 2 hours, turning several times. Remove from marinade, place in rack and broil or bake, basting with marinade and turning 2 or 3 times. Use low heat to avoid burning.

*For Beef:* Marinate steaks or brochettes of beef at least 24 hours. Broil or sauté in a pan, basting with marinade during cooking.

# Antlers Plaza Hotel

This modern hostelry in Colorado Springs, Colorado, has a relaxed holiday atmosphere. Its London Grill is famous for its international cuisine. The Grill is open weekdays for lunch and dinner; closed for lunch on weekends; reservations advisable for dinner.

### STEAK DIANA

Season eight 4-oz. filets of beef tenderloin with salt and pepper. Sauté in 2 tbsp. sweet butter to taste. Flambé with brandy. Remove meat from pan, but keep warm.

Add 1 cup sliced scallions, ½ clove garlic and ½ tbsp. crushed black pepper to pan juices and sauté together for a minute or two or until onions are transparent. Add 8 to 10 oz. dry sherry and reduce sauce until it thickens slightly. Add 1 tbsp. sweet butter. Top steak with sauce. Serves 4.

Above: Malio's Restaurant, Santa Cruz, California (painting by Robert Taylor); right: Colonial Inn, Trinidad, California (painting by Ralph Hulett); lower right: House of Garner, Ukiah, California (painting by Lou McMurray); below: Antlers Plaza Hotel, Colorado Springs, Colorado (painting by Frank Saso)

# Cork 'n Cleaver

The short menu is printed on a meat cleaver and the wine list is printed on a Jeroboam wine bottle in this delightful Spanish-style restaurant at 925 South 8th Street in Colorado Springs, Colorado. The specialty of the house is aged beef broiled over open charcoal grills. From I-25 take Cimmeron Exit and go 4 blocks to 8th Street, turn south on 8th Street and go 1 mile to the restaurant. Open for dinner every day. Reservations not accepted. Closed Thanksgiving, Christmas Eve and Christmas Day.

### TERIYAKI SIRLOIN

8 aged top sirloin steaks (12 oz. each)
23-oz. can pineapple juice     1¼ cups soy sauce
1½ cups burgundy wine
1 rounded tsp. ground ginger

Mix ingredients (except steaks) with wire whip and pour into a deep pot or bowl. Place steaks in marinade, fat side up. Marinate to taste—12 hours minimum, 24 hours maximum. Remove meat, place in clean container and seal from outside air until ready to be cooked. Broil steaks to individual taste over charcoal fire or under oven broiler. (Don't use marinade a second time—it loses its distinctive flavor.)

# The Broadmoor

A world-famous resort, this luxury hotel is surrounded by a 5,000-acre playground which offers a wide variety of year-round recreation. Dining is equally varied—from the Penrose Room which fills the top floor of the Broadmoor South to steak fries held once a week in nearby Fishers Canyon. Take U.S. 85 and 87 south from Colorado Springs to State Highway 122 and the hotel. Reservations necessary for rooms and meals.

## VERMONT CHRISTMAS GOOSE, COLONEL SCHIFFELER

1 oven-ready 8- to 12-lb. goose
1 lb. chopped onion      1 cup goose fat
6 apples, peeled and sliced      6 eggs
1 quart sauterne      1 tbsp. salt
⅛ tsp. pepper      ⅛ tsp. thyme
2 lb. dry rolls, crumbled, or 1 loaf dry white bread

Soak the goose overnight in water with a little salt, drain. To prepare stuffing, sauté onions in goose fat; add apples. Remove from fire when apples are tender-crisp.

Beat eggs into sauterne, add salt, pepper and thyme, and pour over crumbled rolls. Let rolls absorb wine mixture, add cooked onions and apples, stuff goose and sew up cavity. Roast at 375° for 4½ to 5 hours, basting occasionally.

# Normandy French Restaurant

Provincial France provides the décor for this restaurant which is noted for its excellent cuisine, superb service, and one of the finest wine selections in the Denver area. Open the year around, for lunch and dinner Monday through Friday; dinner only Saturday, Sunday and holidays. The address is East Colfax Avenue at Madison Street (U.S 36 and 40), Denver. Reservations required.

### COQ AU VIN ROUGE

Cut two 2½-lb. frying chickens in pieces. Rub pieces with 1 tsp. salt, ½ tsp. white pepper, 2 chopped shallots (or onion), and 1 clove chopped garlic. Dip into flour, coating chicken thoroughly.

Preheat 1 cup vegetable oil to smoking point in a heavy skillet. Add chicken and fry until golden brown on all sides. Remove and pour drippings from skillet into pot; add 1 quart chicken consommé, 2 tbsp. Kitchen Bouquet, 1 No. 2½ can tomatoes, and bouquet garni (herb bunch). Bring to a boil. Thicken with either flour or cornstarch to consistency of sauce or gravy.

Add chicken pieces and cook in sauce until done—about 45 minutes. Add 2 cups burgundy wine after chicken has cooked 20 minutes. Ten minutes before the chicken is done add 1 can tiny whole onions, 1 lb. canned or fresh mushrooms (sauté fresh mushrooms first) and ½ cup diced fried bacon.

Left: The Broadmoor, Colorado Springs, Colorado (painting by Don Bennett); lower left: Normandy French Restaurant, Denver, Colorado (painting by Bill Deno); below: Cork 'n Cleaver, Colorado Springs, Colorado (painting by Bill Kaston)

# Sperte's Laffite

A breath of old New Orleans in the shadow of the Rockies, this popular French restaurant at 14th and Larimer in downtown Denver is open for lunch and dinner weekdays; closed on Sunday. Reservations necessary. There is entertainment nightly in the main dining room.

### POMPANO EN PAPILLOTE

4 fillets of pompano (or red snapper
or striped bass), 4 oz.each
¼ lb. butter        ½ tsp. chopped parsley
3 scallops        1 clove garlic, chopped fine
3 jumbo shrimp, diced        ½ onion, chopped fine
2 large mushrooms, diced
1½ tsp. flour        1 cup consommé

Heat butter in skillet, add remaining ingredients except flour and consommé. Simmer gently for 10 minutes. Cut 4 pieces of brown paper or aluminum foil into 8x10-inch pieces. Brush each with melted butter on one side. Gently remove pompano from sauce.

To sauce in skillet now add flour and consommé. Cook for 5 minutes. Ladle a spoonful of sauce on each square, place portions of fish in sauce and pour remaining sauce over the 4 portions. Fold paper securely and bake at 350° for 15 minutes. Serve in pouches and let each guest unwrap his own.

# Clock Tower Inn

A year-round vacation resort at Gore Creek Drive and Bridge Street in Vail, Colorado, this hostelry is a popular rendezvous for après ski and indoor and outdoor dining according to season. Closed April 15 to June 1.

### CLOCK TOWER CAESAR SALAD

Rub a chilled salad bowl with a garlic bud, then add 2 heads of romaine lettuce cut in pieces. Dribble ½ cup salad oil over greens, add 1 raw egg and toss lightly.

Add ⅓ cup wine vinegar, the juice of a small lemon, 1 tbsp. Worcestershire Sauce, ½ cup grated Parmesan cheese and salt and pepper to taste; toss again. Add 1 cup crisp croutons. Serve immediately on large chilled salad plates. Serves 8.

# Red Lion Inn

In winter this is where the ski trails—and the skiers—meet; in summer, guests can dine outdoors on the Red Lion's canopied terrace. It is in Vail, Colorado. Open 11:30 a.m. to 10 p.m. every day in winter; closed Tuesdays in summer and all during May.

### AVOCADO PEARS RED LION INN

In a heavy saucepan melt 4 tbsp. butter. Stir in 1 tbsp. chopped shallots or onions and sauté lightly. Add 1½ lb. Alaskan King crabmeat and heat, stirring with wooden spoon, until liquid is nearly all evaporated.

Sprinkle with 1½ tsp. paprika and blend in ⅓ cup dry sherry and ⅓ cup cognac; simmer for 5 minutes until liquid is again reduced. Sprinkle with 2 tbsp. flour and stir well. Blend in ½ cup whipping cream and simmer, stirring, for 3 to 5 minutes until mixture thickens. Add 2 tbsp. lemon juice and season to taste with cayenne pepper, garlic, mace, salt, white pepper and Ac'cent (MSG).

Halve 6 avocados, remove pits, place in buttered pan. Stuff with crabmeat mixture. Blend 6 tbsp. whipped cream into 1 cup of hot hollandaise sauce. Pour hot sauce over avocados, sprinkle heavily with Parmesan cheese. Bake at 350° for 10 to 15 minutes or until tops brown. Sprinkle with chopped parsley. Serves 6.

# Ala Moana Hotel

This 1,300-room hotel in Honolulu, Hawaii, commands spectacular views of Diamond Head, sparkling beaches and rolling surf. Its 4 dining rooms include the posh 36th-floor Summit, one of the few places in Hawaii to offer dinner dancing.

### SADDLE OF LAMB WITH PARSLEY

Rub a 4-lb. saddle of lamb with salt and pepper and insert slices of garlic (2 cloves) along underside of joint. Roast on rack, with any additional fat, for 20 minutes at 400°.

Mix 6 oz. white bread crumbs, 2 heaping tbsp. chopped parsley and 5 oz. melted butter together and press thickly all over fat side of meat. Continue roasting for about 40 minutes until meat is cooked and crumbs browned. Make gravy in the usual way. Serves 6.

Upper left: Sperte's Laffite, Denver, Colorado (painting by Phil Hayward); center left: Red Lion Inn, Vail, Colorado (painting by Al Anderson); lower left: Ala Moana Hotel, Honolulu, Hawaii (photo by Camera Hawaii); above: Clock Tower Inn, Vail, Colorado (painting by James Haughey)

# Waioli Tea Room

This is a garden dining room surrounded by magnificent tropical flowers and trees. It is located at 3016 Oahu Avenue in Honolulu, Hawaii. Open every weekday for lunch from 11:30 a.m. to 2 p.m., with "high tea" by reservation only from 2:30 to 4 p.m. Closed Sunday.

### PINEAPPLE BARS

*Filling:*

| | |
|---|---|
| ¼ cup sugar | 1½ cups crushed pineapple |
| 1½ tsp. cornstarch | 3 tsp. guava jam |

Blend sugar and cornstarch. Stir into pineapple with jam. Cook and stir over low heat until clear and thick. (Allow to cool while making crust.)

*Crust:*

| | |
|---|---|
| 1½ cups sifted all-purpose flour | ½ tsp. salt |
| ½ tsp. soda | 1½ cups uncooked rolled oats |
| 1 cup brown sugar | ¾ cup shortening |

Sift together flour, soda and salt. Mix with oats and brown sugar. Work in shortening until mixture is crumbly. Put half of this mixture into 9-inch-square pan, then spread and press filling onto this first layer. Use remaining crumbly mix for top crust. Bake at 375° oven for 40 minutes. Cool in refrigerator until firm. Cut into bars or squares.

# The Royal

The 4 dining rooms in this charming restaurant are decorated in Gay 90s style. Conveniently located in the center of Boise, Idaho, just 2 blocks north of main highways, the Royal is at 1112 Main Street, across the street from the Owyhee Motor Inn. Open every weekday from 11 a.m. to 1 a.m. Closed on Sunday and some holidays.

### FOWL 'N FOIL

Split six 8-oz. chicken breasts, dredge in seasoned flour, brown in 3 tbsp. hot oil. Spread browned chicken in baking pan and cover with mixture of ½ cup sauterne, ¼ tsp. thyme, ½ tsp. white pepper, 1 tsp. salt, and ¼ lb. butter, melted. Bake in 400° oven for 45 minutes or until done.

Remove chicken meat from bones in pieces as large as possible. Prepare 6 squares of heavy foil about 12 inches square. Divide 2 cups wild rice dressing equally and place on foil squares, then place meat of one chicken breast on each square. Top each with: 2 tbsp. chicken gravy; 4 button mushrooms; a little diced pimento and a pinch of parsley flakes.

Fold foil over to make each a tight package. Before serving place in a 275° oven until serving temperature—about 1 hour if packets are cold; 30 minutes if heated immediately after being prepared. Serve in foil packets. Makes 6 portions.

# Hill's Resort and Lodge

This excellent family summer resort is located on Priest Lake in Idaho, in an area of magnificent scenery. Housekeeping cabins as well as rooms in the lodge are available. Open for breakfast, lunch and dinner daily during the season; reservations advisable on weekends. Open from Memorial Day through Labor Day. It is 30 miles north of Priest River by way of State Highway 57; at Route 5 go 3½ miles east to the resort.

### FRESH HUCKLEBERRY GLACE PIE

1 quart huckleberries, washed and drained
¾ cup water
3 tbsp. cornstarch combined with 1 cup sugar
1 tsp. to 1 tbsp. lemon juice, according to berries
9-inch baked pastry shell
Whipped cream or ice cream

Simmer 1 cup of the berries with water for 3 or 4 minutes. Add combined sugar and cornstarch to the cooking fruit. Cook again until syrup is thick and ruby-clear. Stir constantly. When about thickened add lemon juice. Cool slightly.

Line baked pastry shell with 3 cups of uncooked and very well-drained berries. Pour slightly cooled glacé mixture over. Mix in slightly with a fork—very gently. Chill thoroughly. Serve with whipped or ice cream.

### OYSTERS ESCONDIDA

For each serving use about 16 tiny (yearling) oysters. Sauté them in a medium hot skillet containing 1 tsp. butter, 6 tsp. vegetable oil, a shake of garlic salt or 1 small clove garlic (crushed), and a pinch of sweet basil. Season to taste with salt, pepper and Ac'cent (MSG). Serve hot with lime wedges.

Top: Waioli Tea Room, Honolulu, Hawaii (painting by Harvey Kidder); left: The Royal, Boise, Idaho (painting by Don Bennett); below: Hill's Resort and Lodge, Priest Lake, Idaho (painting by Harvey Kidder)

# Bacchanal Room

Among the most celebrated of the myriad eating places in Las Vegas, Nevada, is The Bacchanal. Exquisite dinners are prepared here by master chefs and served by torch-bearing, toga-clad attendants. Overnight accommodations are available at Caesar's Palace, in which the restaurant is located. The address is 3570 Las Vegas Boulevard South. Open for dinner every day. Reservations are necessary.

### VEAL CORDON BLEU

2½ lb. veal
½ lb. prosciutto ham, sliced thin
½ lb. Swiss cheese, sliced thin
5 eggs      1 cup heavy cream
1 cup flour      ¼ lb. butter
2 cups bread or cracker crumbs
Salt and pepper, to taste
2 cups tomato sauce

Slice veal in 16 large thin pieces, pound to ¼ inch thickness or less. Sandwich ham and cheese slices between two veal slices. Beat eggs together with cream. Dip veal sandwiches into flour, then into cream-and-egg mixture and finally in crumbs. Season with salt and pepper, to taste.

Pan-fry veal sandwiches in butter until slightly brown on both sides—about 5 minutes over medium heat. Top with hot tomato sauce. Can be served with noodles blended with rich cream sauce and flavored with Parmesan cheese. Serves 8.

# Hacienda Dining Room

Located on the Old Town Plaza in the historic section of downtown Albuquerque, New Mexico, near I-40, this colorful dining room is famous for its delicious Mexican and American foods served in a Spanish atmosphere. Lunch and dinner every day except Thanksgiving. Reservations are not necessary for Christmas and New Year's Day, but are advisable during the summer months.

### TURKEY OR CHICKEN MOLE

4 slices bread      2 tbsp. fat
1 clove garlic, minced      1 small onion, minced
¼ cup peanuts      ¼ cup almonds
2 tbsp. chili powder      1¼ cups chicken broth
¼ tsp. cinnamon      ¼ tsp. cloves
2 tbsp. brown sugar      2 tbsp. water
½ oz. bitter chocolate      Salt and pepper
1½ lb. sliced roasted chicken or turkey

Sauté bread in fat, then drain and remove. Sauté garlic and onion in the same fat. Grind bread, garlic, onion, and nuts very fine to make a paste. Add chili powder, broth, spices, sugar and water. Bring to a boil, stirring constantly. Add chocolate, stirring until melted. Add salt and pepper, to taste.

Add chicken or turkey slices (cut thin or in small pieces) and simmer about 1 hour until flavors are blended. Makes 6 portions.

# The Compound

Designed by the famous architect Alexander Girard, this is one of the most popular restaurants in historic Santa Fe, New Mexico. It's located at 653 Canyon Road a mile east of the Plaza. Open for lunch and dinner daily except Sunday evening. Reservations are necessary. Victor Sagheers is the owner-manager.

### VEAL PICATTA

1½ lb. veal scallops (very thin slices)
¾ cup seasoned flour      4 oz. butter
½ cup chicken broth      1 cup dry white wine
½ tsp. salt      Freshly ground pepper
1 lemon, sliced thin

Dip each piece of veal into flour, shaking off excess. Heat butter in pan over medium heat. Sauté veal quickly, a few pieces at a time, using about 2 tbsp. of butter for each panful. Remove veal and keep warm.

Pour chicken broth into pan, stir well to pick up browned pieces, then add wine and salt. Cook 1 minute. Return veal to sauce and cook 2 to 3 minutes until bubbly. Sprinkle with freshly ground pepper. Arrange veal on serving platter, pour wine mixture over it and top with lemon slices. Makes 6 portions.

Left: Bacchanal Room, Caesar's Palace, Las Vegas, Nevada (painting by Douglas Snow); lower left: Hacienda Dining Room, Albuquerque, New Mexico (painting by Joel T. Ramirez); below: The Compound, Santa Fe, New Mexico (painting by Jim Prindiville)

## Mon Desir Dining Inn

Excellent service and fine food are the hallmarks of this restaurant in a lovely old country home. Located near Central Point, Oregon, it is east of I-5 and north of Medford. Dinner only, from 6 to 10 p.m. Closed Mondays and Christmas day. Reservations advisable.

### POACHED NORTHWEST SALMON

| | |
|---|---|
| 4 salmon fillets or steaks | Juice of ½ lemon |
| 1½ cups chicken stock | Chopped dill |
| ½ cup white wine | Salt, to taste |

Place salmon in baking dish. Barely cover with combination of remaining ingredients. Poach in 425° oven for 20 minutes. Chill in liquid. Remove to serving platter with spatula. Garnish and serve with tartar sauce. Serve cold. Makes 4 portions.

## Bart's Wharf and Marina

"Tops in view 'n' seafood, too," is the way the Bart Woodyards describe their restaurant which overlooks the Columbia River in Portland, Oregon—but specialties here include charcoal-broiled steaks, as well. The address is 3839 Northeast Marine Drive at 38th Street. Open for lunch and dinner every day except Monday, 11 a.m. to midnight. Reservations not necessary.

### BAKED MAINE LOBSTER

For each 1½-lb. lobster combine the following ingredients into a dressing: 16 crushed butter crackers, ⅛ lb. melted butter, ½ tsp. Ac'cent (MSG), 2 tsp. lemon juice, 1 dash each of Tabasco and Worcestershire sauces; pinch each of thyme and chopped parsley.

Clean raw lobster and fill cavity with dressing. Sprinkle with grated Parmesan cheese; bake at 400° for 20 minutes.

## The London Grill, Benson Hotel

The Benson, a charming old hotel at 309 Southwest Broadway in Portland, Oregon, carries on the traditions of old England in its London Grill, named for the famous 16th-century restaurant which was a favorite of Charles Dickens. Open 6:30 a.m. to 1 a.m. daily.

### ROAST DUCKLING WINDSOR

Split five 5-lb. ducklings and place in a roasting pan on a bed of 3 sliced carrots, 3 stalks celery, chopped, and 3 sliced onions. Season with salt and pepper. Roast in 325° oven for about 60 minutes or until done. Remove from pan and keep warm. Deglaze pan with 4 cups white wine, simmer 5 minutes.

In another pan melt 3 tbsp. butter and add ¾ cup diced almonds. Sauté until golden brown, add 1 cup honey and mix well. Pour 1 jigger Triple Sec over mixture and flame it. Combine with wine drippings and 3½ cups of good brown sauce; simmer until hot. Pour sauce over ducklings on platter. Garnish with nectarine or peach halves. Serve immediately. Makes 10 portions.

## Tumalo Emporium

Tumalo Emporium has deliberately bucked the trend of standardized menus and décor by furnishing its dining room with handsome antique oak tables and chairs, a bar from a Nevada ghost town and other furnishings from "the good old days." This restaurant bakes all of its own breads and desserts, makes its own salad dressings and creates imaginative ice cream specialties which guests may enjoy at an old-fashioned marble-topped soda fountain. There is also a museum that features a typical pioneer home. The Emporium is in Tumalo, Oregon, 6 miles north of Bend, on U.S. 20. Dinners served daily.

### EMPORIUM WALNUT PIE

| | |
|---|---|
| 2 cups sugar | 1 cup water |
| ½ tsp. salt | 1½ sticks butter |
| 1 tsp. vanilla | 9-inch unbaked pie shell |
| 6 yolks from large eggs | |
| 1 cup chopped walnuts | |

Boil sugar, water, and salt together until syrup reaches 235° on a candy thermometer or spins a thread 2 inches long. Add butter; boil until bubbles are all yellow. Cool to room temperature.

Add vanilla and eggs to above mixture and beat thoroughly. Place chopped walnuts on the bottom of a 9-inch unbaked pie shell; pour pie mixture over them. Bake for 55 minutes at 325° or until pie is set and a glossy light brown on top.

Top: Mon Desir Dining Inn, Central Point, Oregon (painting by Marcus Hamilton); above: The London Grill, Benson Hotel, Portland, Oregon (painting by John Waddingham); upper right: Bart's Wharf and Marina, Portland, Oregon (painting by John Waddingham); right: Tumalo Emporium, Tumalo, Oregon (painting by Max Altekruse)

# Royce's Restaurant

Royce Roosendaal is the owner of this restaurant in Salt Lake City, Utah, which is decorated in a nostalgic mood with old family portraits, gas lamps and other antiques. For 18 years diners have been enjoying such house specialties as frog legs meunière, veal cordon bleu and a selection of delightfully rich desserts. Take 13th East ramp from I-80 and proceed to 3680 Highland Drive.

### CARAMEL PECAN PIE

| | |
|---|---|
| 4 eggs, slightly beaten | 1 cup sugar |
| Pinch of salt | 1 cup dark Karo syrup |
| 1 tsp. vanilla | 3 tbsp. melted butter |
| 1 cup pecan halves | 8-inch unbaked pie shell |

Beat eggs slightly, then add sugar, salt, corn syrup, vanilla and melted butter. Place pecans in bottom of pie shell and pour filling over them. Bake in a very hot, 450° oven for 15 minutes. Reduce heat to 350° and bake about 35 more minutes, or until knife inserted in the center of the pie comes out clean.

# Andy's Diner

Railroad buffs especially will enjoy Andy's Diner for it's housed in 6 old railroad cars and boasts authentic railroad antiques and an outstanding selection of railroad pictures. It's open for lunch and dinner 11:30 a.m. to midnight every day except Sunday and holidays. The address is 2963 Fourth Avenue South in Seattle, Washington.

### ANDY'S BLUE CHEESE DRESSING

| | |
|---|---|
| ½ tsp. garlic powder or 1 clove garlic, crushed | |
| ¼ cup buttermilk | 1 tsp. onion salt |
| 2½ cups mayonnaise | 1 tsp. parsley flakes |
| 1 tsp. whole oregano | 1 tsp. Ac'cent (MSG) |
| 1 cup blue cheese, crumbled | 3 tsp. sugar |
| 1 tsp. celery seed | ½ cup cottage cheese |
| 1 tsp. black pepper | ½ tsp. salt |

Combine all ingredients and mix well. Makes approximately 1 quart.

# Clark's Windjammer

This restaurant offers the best in Northwest seafoods as well as a panoramic view of a vast pleasure boat marina, Puget Sound and the Olympic Mountains. Open daily for lunch and dinner until 11:30 p.m. The Top Cabin Lounge offers dancing and entertainment until 2 a.m. every weekday, and is open Sunday 2 to 10 p.m. Closed Christmas Day. Reservations advisable. From I-5 take 85th Street Exit. The restaurant is at 7001 Seaview Avenue, N.W., Seattle, Washington.

### NOODLES AU TIM

Cook 8 oz. long, medium-thick egg noodles in boiling, salted water for 10 minutes. Wash in cold water.

Combine 2 cups sour cream, 2 cups cottage cheese, 1 clove garlic (minced), 1 tsp. Worcestershire Sauce, a dash of Tabasco, ¼ cup chopped onion, ¼ cup butter, and salt and pepper to taste. Combine this mixture with noodles and pour into greased casserole. Bake 45 minutes at 350°. Serve with grated Parmesan cheese. Serves 8.

# Rosellini's Four-10

This restaurant takes its name from its address: 410 University Street in downtown Seattle, Washington. Meals served every weekday from 11 a.m. to midnight; Saturday 5 p.m. to midnight. Closed Sundays and holidays. Chef Robert Carson, who presides over the kitchen, is only 30 years old, but is celebrated in the Pacific Northwest for his culinary talents. Reservations necessary. Victor Rosellini is the owner.

### PEARS BELLE HELENA

| | |
|---|---|
| 1 cup hot chocolate sauce | |
| 4 scoops vanilla ice cream | |
| 8 Bartlett pear halves | 1 cup whipped cream |
| 4 tbsp. green crème de menthe | |
| 4 stemmed maraschino cherries | |
| 4 sprigs fresh mint | Sugar wafers |

Place 2 tsp. chocolate sauce in each of 4 hollow stemmed coupe glasses. Place scoop of ice cream in each. Arrange 2 pear halves cut side down on opposite sides of ice cream. Pour remaining chocolate sauce over pears and ice cream. Place 2 whipped cream rosettes between each pear half and a large swirl of whipped cream on top of ice cream. Garnish with crème de menthe, mint sprig and cherry. Serve with sugar wafer. Serves 4.

Upper left: Royce's Restaurant, Salt Lake City, Utah (painting by Douglas Snow); lower left: Clark's Windjammer, Seattle, Washington (painting by James Peck); upper right: Andy's Diner, Seattle, Washington (painting by Harry Bonath); lower right: Rosellini's Four-10, Seattle, Washington (painting by Rudolph Bundas)

# Victor's 610 Restaurant

For over 20 years this Italian restaurant in downtown Seattle, Washington, at 610 Pine Street has provided a congenial atmosphere as well as excellent food. Open for lunch and dinner every weekday; closed on Sunday and holidays. Reservations advisable.

## MINESTRONE

1 cup dried navy beans        4 peppercorns
1 tbsp. salt        1 cup finely chopped onion
1 cup chopped celery with leaves
1 garlic clove, minced        ½ cup olive oil
2½ cups canned tomatoes
¼ cup chopped parsley
2 cups shredded cabbage
1 zucchini, sliced thin
1 cup cut macaroni        Grated Parmesan cheese

Soak beans in 8 cups of water overnight. Bring to a boil in the same water, reduce heat, add salt and peppercorns, cover and simmer for 1 hour. Sauté celery, onion, and garlic in olive oil for 10 minutes or until onion is lightly browned. Add to beans with tomato and parsley. Bring to a boil, reduce heat, cover and simmer for 1 hour.

Add cabbage, zucchini, and macaroni, and simmer uncovered for 15 minutes, stirring occasionally. Serve with grated Parmesan cheese. Serves 6.

# Restaurant Continental

This restaurant is at Snoqualmie Pass, on I-90 in Washington, in the spectacular Cascade Mountains. It's part of Alpenhaus, a year-round resort. Open every day for lunch and dinner; reservations advised on weekends.

## FROMAGE FONDUE À LA SUISSE

Heat 2 cups Rhine wine in a double boiler. Add 1 lb. Swiss cheese, cubed, stir in with wire whip. Add ⅛ tsp. white pepper, ⅛ tsp. garlic powder and ⅛ tsp. nutmeg and stir until smooth. Thicken sauce with 1 tbsp. cornstarch dissolved in a little cold water. Add ¼ cup kirsch.

Serve in heavy fondue pot kept hot with table heater. Give each diner a long-handled fork and a supply of French bread cut in large cubes to dunk and swirl in the fondue. Serves 4.

# Davenport Hotel

Dining in the gracious atmosphere of old-time hotel-keeping is a tradition in the Matador Room of the Davenport Hotel, at 807 West Sprague Street, Spokane, Washington, 3 blocks south of I-90. Open for lunch and dinner every day except Sunday, with entertainment at night.

## ROAST DUCKLING DAVENPORT

Stuff a 5-lb. duckling with fresh parsley and a slice of ginger root the size of a quarter. Truss it and season with salt and pepper. Place it on a rack, breast side up, in a roasting pan; add 1 cup water. Arrange aluminum foil loosely over the top and roast at 550° for 45 minutes.

Remove foil; pour off excess grease. Pour ½ cup sherry into the duck cavity and continue roasting at 325° for 30 minutes or until done. Remove from pan and remove parsley and ginger root from cavity. While duckling is still hot, cut into thin slices and serve with plum sauce (below).

*Plum Sauce:* Combine 1 cup granulated sugar, 1 cup white vinegar, 1 cup water and 4 tbsp. cornstarch; bring to a boil. Add 1 cup Chinese plum sauce and 1 piece ginger root the size of a quarter. Simmer 10 minutes.

# Sheridan Center Inn

Just a 20-minute drive from the famed Big Horn Mountains on I-90 in Sheridan, Wyoming, this modern motor hotel offers the vacationing family 2 swimming pools, excellent fishing, camping and backpacking. Breakfast, lunch and dinner served daily. The address is 609 North Main Street.

## VEAL SCALLOPINI

Have 2 lb. boneless veal cut into 1¼-oz. pieces. Roll in French bread crumbs and brown in 2 oz. olive oil. To the pan, add 2 oz. each of sliced mushrooms, chopped green peppers, chopped onions and chopped celery. Add 4 oz. crushed tomatoes; simmer for 10 minutes.

Then add 2 oz. sherry, 2 cups brown sauce, salt and pepper to taste. Simmer for an additional 10 minutes.

Boil 2 lb. very thin spaghetti. Serve the meat at the side and pour sauce over spaghetti. Makes 8 portions.

Upper left: Restaurant Continental, Snoqualmie Pass, Washington (painting by Robert Blanchard); lower left: Sheridan Center Inn, Sheridan, Wyoming (painting by Glen S. Hopkinson); upper right: Victor's 610 Restaurant, Seattle, Washington (illustration by Jim Krechnyak); lower right: Davenport Hotel, Spokane, Washington (painting by Rudolph Bundas)

# Canada

Broad land of contrasts that it is, Canada has developed a widely varying cuisine, from the simple, hearty dishes of its Northern and Western frontiers to the long-perfected delicacies of Eastern provinces whose roots go back to the 17th century. F. Wenderoth Saunders' painting of a herring wharf is the background for an assortment of Canada's many seafoods, cheeses, fruits and wines.

135

# Château Lacombe

The memory of Father Albert Lacombe, pioneer missionary, is perpetuated in this spectacular new circular hotel tower overlooking the North Saskatchewan River in downtown Edmonton, Alberta. Shown here is the informal Chevalier Grill, the main dining room at the luxurious hotel. Reservations advisable.

## ARCTIC CHAR À LA MEUNIÈRE

8 thick arctic char steaks
(or salmon or lake trout)
1 cup white wine      2 bay leaves
1 cup court bouillon      Bouquet garni
8 peppercorns      1 clove garlic, mashed
1 lemon, juice and rind
1 tsp. Worcestershire Sauce
1 leek (white part only)      1 small onion
½ cup butter      2 anchovy fillets

Cut the fish into steaks, wipe and salt. Boil in white wine combined with court bouillon (the liquid must cover the fish). Add to the liquid a bouquet garni, bay leaves, peppercorns, garlic, juice of the lemon and Worcestershire Sauce. Simmer until fish is tender, about 15 minutes.

Chop the leek, onion, anchovies and lemon rind. Add butter. Heat the mixture, stirring constantly, and cook until golden brown. Place fish on platter, remove center bone and skin. Cover with the above mixture and serve with sour cream sauce (below).

*Sour Cream Sauce:* Melt 3 tbsp. butter over low heat, stir in 4 tbsp. flour, mix until smooth. Add 2½ cups milk gradually, stirring well. Add 3 tbsp. butter, ½ cup sour cream, ½ tsp. sugar and salt to taste. Boil a few minutes, then add 2 tbsp. sherry. Serve hot over char steaks.

# Timber Club Restaurant, Hotel Vancouver

The Timber Club Restaurant in the Hotel Vancouver honors lumbering with a décor that includes 38 matched Douglas fir logs festooned with foliage. The restaurant is open every weekday for lunch and dinner; dinner only served on Sunday. Reservations recommended for meals and hotel accommodations. The address is 900 West Georgia Street in downtown Vancouver, British Columbia.

## SALMON AU CHAMPAGNE

2-lb. salmon fillet (in one piece)      4 oz. butter
5 chopped shallots      4 large mushroom caps
8 oz. dry champagne      6 oz. heavy cream
Salt, pepper and lemon to taste

Melt butter in a shallow oven pan and add chopped shallots. Place salmon on top. Arrange mushroom caps on salmon, pour champagne over it, cover with buttered paper, and bring to a boil over a burner. Place pan in hot oven (375°) and poach 10 or 15 minutes until done.

Remove poached salmon, discard paper covering; add cream to champagne remaining in the pan, and reduce this liquid to half its volume over a medium fire. Season to taste, strain sauce and pour over fish. Serves 6.

# The Empress Hotel

One of Canada's finest, this resort hotel is surrounded by gardens overlooking the harbor in Victoria, British Columbia. Within minutes of the hotel, which is in the heart of the city at 721 Government Street, are such attractions as golfing on tournament courses, sailing, and fishing for world-famous tyee salmon. During the winter the Empress Dining Room is open only for dinner; in summer it is open for breakfast, lunch and dinner. The Coffee Shop is open for all 3 meals, year around. Overnight accommodations and vacation facilities.

## QUICHE LORRAINE

3 oz. bacon      1 medium onion, diced
2 tbsp. mushrooms, chopped
2 tsp. chopped parsley      2 oz. Gruyère cheese
3 oz. aged Canadian cheese
1 pint light cream      4 beaten eggs
Dash of garlic salt, white pepper and nutmeg
9-inch unbaked pie shell

Sauté bacon, onion, mushrooms and parsley, drain off excess fat, and let cool. Cut both kinds of cheese into small cubes, combine with sautéed ingredients and place in pie shell.

Combine cream, beaten eggs and seasonings and pour into pie shell. Bake in 400° oven for 10 minutes, reduce heat to 350° and continue baking for another 30 minutes. Serve warm. Makes 6 portions.

Upper left: Château La-
combe, Edmonton, Alberta
(painting by Dick Bobnick);
left: Timber Club Restaurant,
Hotel Vancouver, British
Columbia (painting by Jim
Krechnyak); above: The Empress Hotel, Victoria, British
Columbia (painting by Craw-
ford Livingston)

# The Fire Hall Restaurant

This 3-floor restaurant and entertainment complex is housed in Toronto's oldest fire hall, which was built in 1886. The place is adorned with fire-fighting memorabilia. There is even a 1930 fire engine. Open for lunch and dinner every weekday; closed Sundays. A discotheque—the Fire Escape—is open 8 p.m. to midnight. Reservations advisable. At 110 Lombard Street.

## FRENCH DRESSED CANTALOUPE

This is a specialty of Engine Company No. 10, San Francisco. Cut 2 medium-sized cantaloupes in half crosswise and remove seeds. With a melon cutter, scoop melon balls into a bowl. Smooth inside of shells, chill.

Cut 2 medium-sized tomatoes into thin wedges; dice half a green pepper; cut 3 green onions, including part of green tops, into thin slices; then combine these 3 ingredients with melon balls and pour ½ cup oil and vinegar French dressing over them. Cover and chill for 4 hours. Heap marinated mixture into chilled cantaloupe shells. Serves 4 as a salad or appetizer.

# Walker House Hotel

This downtown Toronto hotel has 3 award-winning restaurants. The elegant Franz Josef Room features Austrian cuisine in a Viennese atmosphere, with dancing and entertainment nightly. Superb German foods are served for lunch and dinner every day except Sunday in the Rathskeller, which also has dinner music nightly. The Swiss Bear is a congenial hideaway which is open for lunch and light refreshments in the late afternoon and evening. Reservations advisable for hotel rooms and meals. The address is 121 Front Street.

## JUMBO SHRIMP MIGNONETTE

24 large shrimp, peeled and deveined
2 tsp. butter     2 tsp. olive oil
2 tsp. chopped onions
⅛ tsp. chopped parsley
⅛ tsp. chopped garlic
Chopped tarragon leaves
Salt and pepper to taste
3 oz. dry white wine     ½ cup bread crumbs

Heat butter and oil in skillet. Add onions, parsley, garlic and tarragon and sauté lightly.

Add shrimp and salt and pepper. Add white wine and bring to a boil. Place shrimp and sauce in 4 individual ovenproof platters. Bake at 400° about 5 minutes. Place bread crumbs on top, put the dishes under the broiler until brown. Serves 4.

## FILET GOULASH STROGANOFF

24 oz. lean beef tenderloin     2 tsp. paprika
Salt and pepper to taste
2 tbsp. finely chopped onion     1 oz. oil
½ cup sliced mushrooms     1 tbsp. butter
1 oz. dry white wine     1 cup brown gravy
½ cup sour cream     1 medium-sized dill pickle
Buttered noodles or rice pilaf

Cut meat into ½- to 1½-inch strips, add paprika and salt and pepper to taste. Heat oil and butter in heavy skillet and sauté meat about 2 minutes. Remove meat, cook onions, then add mushrooms and smother slightly.

Add wine to pan, blend with drippings; reduce heat, add gravy and bring to a boil. Turn to low heat, slowly add sour cream (slightly warmed), stir until smooth. Put meat into sauce; add dill pickle, peeled and cut in fine strips; season to taste. Serve with buttered egg noodles or rice pilaf. Serves 4.

# Holiday Inn, Windsor

Perched just a few feet above the Detroit River, the main dining rooms of this restaurant in Windsor, Ontario, afford a spectacular view of the Detroit skyline, as well as a fascinating close-range glimpse of the steady stream of freighters and pleasure craft passing by. Breakfast, buffet lunch and dinner served daily, as well as a buffet dinner on Saturday evenings. Reservations advisable. Overnight accommodations and recreation facilities. The inn is just a few minutes from downtown Detroit by way of the Detroit-Windsor Tunnel, at 480 Riverside Drive West. John Brezsnyak is the Innkeeper.

## STUFFED TOMATOES, ESSEX COUNTY

Halve 3 large tomatoes and remove some of the pulp. Prepare 1½ cup poultry stuffing with liquid as directed on package, add ¼ cup chopped onion and ¼ cup chopped walnuts. Stuff tomato halves.

Beat 2 egg yolks and pour a little on top of each tomato. Then sprinkle ½ cup grated Parmesan cheese over tomatoes and drizzle tops with 4 tbsp. melted butter. Bake in 350° oven for 10 minutes. Serves 6.

Top: The Fire Hall Restaurant, Toronto, Ontario (painting by Huntley Brown); left: Walker House Hotel, Toronto, Canada (painting by Bill Kaston); lower left: Holiday Inn, Windsor, Ontario (painting by Robert Taylor)

# Chez Pauze

A seafood lover's dream, this friendly restaurant has specialized in seafood for over 100 years. It is at 1657 St. Catherine Street West in downtown Montreal. Lunch and dinner served every day except Monday. Reservations necessary. Closed the last week in July and first week of August. Owners Mark and Leonard Astic maintain that the most important rule to remember in cooking fresh fish is to stick to simple methods and make sure the timing is exact. Fish should never be undercooked or overcooked.

## LOBSTER NEWBURG

2 lb. cooked, bite-size chunks lobster meat
½ lb. butter      1 soup spoon dry mustard
1 tsp. Worcestershire Sauce      2 tbsp. cornstarch
½ cup dry white wine      1 quart cream

Melt butter in a pan, add mustard, Worcestershire Sauce and wine. Cook lobster pieces in this mixture about 10 minutes or until pieces have turned red. Add cream and heat gently—do not boil. Add cornstarch moistened with water and stir until thick.

## SCALLOPS WRAPPED IN BACON

Wrap 16 large scallops in raw bacon. Secure with a toothpick. Bake in 500° oven for 10 minutes. Serve as an appetizer for 4.

# Chez Rabelais

This is one of Quebec City's newest restaurants in one of its oldest houses. Halfway up Breakneck Steps between Lower Town and Upper Town at 2 Petit Champlain, it is located in a 250-year-old mansion. The restaurateur, Guy Morin, and his charming wife came from Chinon, France, and serve that region's cuisine. The restaurant's interior has been restored in the somewhat severe style of the 17th century, with original oak beams and furniture of the period. Open every day for lunch and dinner. Reservations necessary.

## FRESH CREAM OF HERRING SOUP

5 fresh herrings, cleaned      Pinch of saffron
2 garlic cloves, mashed      Pinch of clove
2 large onions      2 tbsp. cooking oil
1 leek      1 carrot      10 cups water
½ cup whipping cream      4 tbsp. butter
4 tbsp. flour      2 pieces celery
2 eggs yolks      Salt and pepper, to taste

Cut leek, onions, carrot and celery in large pieces and sauté in hot oil, stirring, until golden. Add herrings, garlic, spices and salt and pepper to taste. Add water and bring to a boil. Cook 15 to 20 minutes on high heat. Strain, reserving bouillon and herrings.

Prepare a roux by melting butter and gradually adding flour while stirring. Add bouillon to roux gradually, stirring constantly until mixture thickens.

Just before serving beat egg yolks into cream and pour into a tureen. Add herrings and thickened bouillon, then stir. Serve with croutons. Makes 8 portions.

# Le Vendome

Halfway between Lower Town and Upper Town in colorful Quebec City, this fine old French restaurant is located at 36 Côte de la Montagne. It is noted for outstanding food served in beautiful surroundings. The pleasant dining room is decorated with murals depicting scenes in the south of France. Lunch and dinner served daily, 11:30 a.m. to 10:30 p.m. The owner, Georges LaHaut, requests that reservations be made during the summer months.

## LE SABAYON

4 tbsp. Grand Marnier (orange-flavored brandy)
4 egg yolks      8 tbsp. white wine
8 tbsp. fine granulated sugar

Combine all ingredients and place in top of a double boiler. Heat, stirring continuously with a whip until thick, about 4 minutes.

Serve immediately with champagne fingers or petits four. Serves 4.

## VEAL CUTLET ROMAINE

Use 2 thinly sliced 2-oz. veal cutlets per person. On 1 slice place a piece of partly cooked bacon or ham, and a slice of Swiss cheese. Top with another slice of veal and skewer with food picks. Make one "sandwich" per serving.

In a bowl prepare a light pancake mixture with white flour. Season with salt and pepper. Dip prepared cutlets in mixture, then sauté in oil. Remove from pan and sauté in butter.

Place in 350° oven for 10 minutes. Serve topped with tomato sauce lightly seasoned with cognac.

Upper left: Chez Rabelais, Quebec City, Quebec (illustration by Al Stelma); lower left: Chez Pauze, Montreal, Quebec (painting by John Walsh); above: Le Vendome, Quebec City, Quebec (painting by John Walsh)

# Recipe Index